Other Books by Bill Watterson

Something Under the Bed Is Drooling
Yukon Ho!
Weirdos from Another Planet
The Revenge of the Baby-Sat
Scientific Progress Goes "Boink"
Attack of the Deranged Mutant Killer Monster Snow Goons
The Days Are Just Packed
Homicidal Psycho Jungle Cat
The Tenth Anniversary

Treasury Collections

The Essential Calvin and Hobbes
The Calvin and Hobbes Lazy Sunday Book
The Authoritative Calvin and Hobbes
The Indispensable Calvin and Hobbes

Calvin and Hobbes

by Bill Watterson

WARNER BOOKS

A Warner Book

First published in the US by Andrews and McMeel 1987
Published by Sphere Books Ltd 1988
Reprinted 1989, 1990 (three times), 1991 (twice), 1992
Reprinted by Warner Books 1995

ISBN 0 7515 1655 4

Printed and bound in Great Britain by
BPC Hazell Books Ltd
A member of
The British Printing Company Ltd

Warner Books
A Division of
Little, Brown and Company (UK)
Brettenham House
Lancaster Place
London WC2E 7EN

TO
MELissa

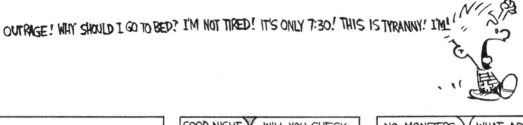

ANY MONSTERS UNDER MY BED TONIGHT?!

NOPE!

NO! UH-UH.

WELL, THERE'D BETTER **NOT** BE! I'D HATE TO HAVE TO **TORCH** ONE WITH MY FLAME THROWER!

YOU HAVE A FLAME THROWER??

THEY LIE. I LIE.

MOM, CAN I DRIVE ON THE WAY BACK?

OF COURSE NOT, CALVIN.

CAN I JUST STEER THEN? I PROMISE I WON'T CRASH.

NO, CALVIN.

CAN I WORK THE GAS AND BRAKES WHILE **YOU** STEER?

NO, CALVIN.

YOU NEVER LET ME DO ANYTHING.

HERE WE FIND A THRIVING CITY: BRAND NEW BUILDINGS, A BUSTLING ECONOMY.

A SCENIC THOROUGHFARE WINDS THROUGH THIS HAPPY MUNICIPALITY. HERE, A FARMER DRIVES HIS LIVESTOCK TO MARKET.

TRAGICALLY, THIS SERENE METROPOLIS LIES DIRECTLY BENEATH THE HOOVER DAM...

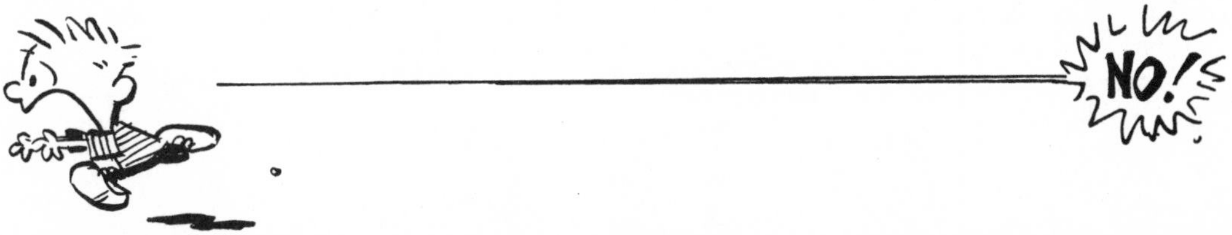

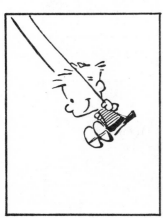

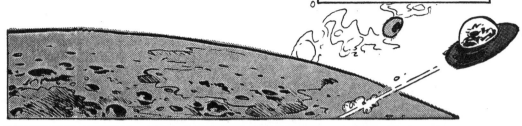

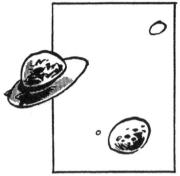

18

 CALVIN, ARE YOU GOING TO TAKE THAT STUFFED TIGER TO SCHOOL AGAIN? SURE.

 DON'T THE KIDS MAKE FUN OF YOU? TOMMY CHESNUTT DID ONCE, AND NOW NOBODY DOES.

 WHY, WHAT HAPPENED TO TOMMY CHESNUTT?

 HOBBES ATE HIM! UGH! HE NEEDED A BATH, TOO...

 CALVIN! WHAT'S ALL THIS NOISE?! YOU'RE SUPPOSED TO BE ASLEEP!

 MONSTERS UNDER THE BED, DAD! I WAS WHACKING ONE WITH MY BASEBALL BAT!

 GOODNESS CALVIN, IT'S JUST YOUR STUFFED TIGER! YOU SHOULD PUT AWAY YOUR TOYS!

 SORRY, OL' BUDDY. GOOD THING I MISSED OCCASIONALLY, HUH? YEAH. LET ME SEE YOUR BAT A MINUTE.

 HERE COMES THE SPORTS CAR AT 200 MILES PER HOUR!

 HERE COMES A CEMENT TRUCK! LOOK OUT!

 AND HERE COMES AN INFLAMMABLE CHEMICAL TRUCK! OH NO!!

 THIS OUGHT TO BE GOOD.

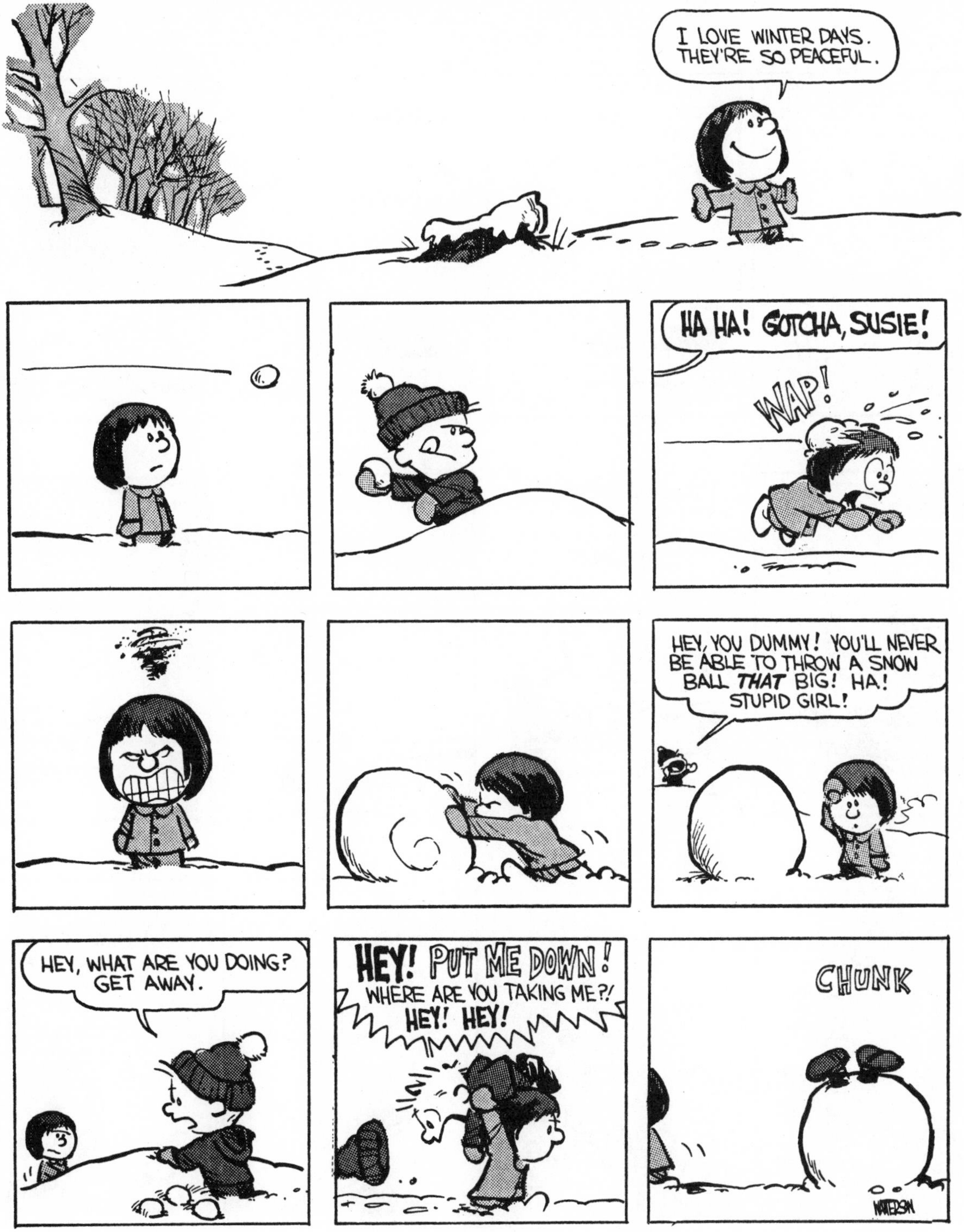
I LOVE WINTER DAYS. THEY'RE SO PEACEFUL.
HA HA! GOTCHA, SUSIE!
WAP!
HEY, YOU DUMMY! YOU'LL NEVER BE ABLE TO THROW A SNOW BALL THAT BIG! HA! STUPID GIRL!
HEY, WHAT ARE YOU DOING? GET AWAY.
HEY! PUT ME DOWN! WHERE ARE YOU TAKING ME?! HEY! HEY!
CHUNK
WATERSON

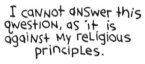

28

WE ARE A FIERCE AND DIRTY BAND OF CUTTHROAT PIRATES!

KEEP A SHARP LOOKOUT, MATEY. WE WANT NO SISSY GIRLS ON OUR SHIP!

WE DON'T *LIKE* GIRLS?

OF COURSE NOT, DUMMY! WE'RE A MURDEROUS BUNCH OF *PIRATES*, REMEMBER?!

WHO DO WE SMOOCH THEN?

WHAT DID YOU BRING FOR SHOW AND TELL, SUSIE?

I BROUGHT A LETTER I WROTE TO OUR CONGRESSMAN.

WHAT DID YOU BRING?

A BAG OF DEAD BUGS I COLLECTED FROM OUR WINDOW SILLS.

BEST OF ALL, THIS WAY MOM DIDN'T HAVE TO PACK ME A LUNCH!

WELL, HOBBES, WE DID IT AGAIN. WE'RE SEPARATED FROM THE TROOP AND HOPELESSLY LOST.

FORTUNATELY, OUR MOTTO IS "BE PREPARED."

WITH THIS FULL BACKPACK, WE CAN STAY OUT HERE FOR WEEKS!

JUST SO LONG AS WE DON'T GET HUNGRY.

29

CALVIN, I DON'T WANT TO BE SPANKED!

WHAT IF IT GOES ON OUR ACADEMIC TRANSCRIPTS? WE'LL BE RUINED!

* SNIFF *

DARN YOU, CALVIN !! YOU'RE GONNA ANSWER TO MY PARENTS IF I CAN'T GET MY MASTER'S DEGREE!

CALVIN AND SUSIE, WOULD YOU COME IN MY OFFICE, PLEASE?

PRINCI

IT WAS ALL HIS FAULT, MR. SPITTLE!

THAT'S A LIE! SHE STARTED IT!

ARE YOU GOING TO SPANK US ??

I'LL NEVER PASS NOTES AGAIN! DON'T SPANK US !!

WAAAHHHH !! I WISH WE WERE DEAD !!

I HATE THIS JOB.

NOW I WANT YOU BOTH TO PAY BETTER ATTENTION IN CLASS, UNDERSTOOD?

YES SIR.

OKAY, YOU MAY RETURN TO YOUR ROOM NOW.

THANK YOU, MR. SPITTLE.

CALVIN? YOU MAY RETURN TO YOUR ROOM.

CALVIN?

THE ZORG DRAWS NEARER. SPIFF SETS HIS BLASTER ON "MEDIUM WELL"...

IT SAYS HERE THAT "RELIGION IS THE OPIATE OF THE MASSES." ...WHAT DO YOU SUPPOSE *THAT* MEANS?

..IT MEANS KARL MARX HADN'T SEEN ANYTHING YET..

WHAT ARE YOU WATCHING?

GARBAGE. THIS SHOW WOULD INSULT A 6-YEAR-OLD! AND I SHOULD KNOW.

SO WHY WATCH IT?

ALL THE OTHER SHOWS ARE EVEN WORSE!

WHY WATCH TV AT ALL THEN?

THERE'S NOTHING TO DO.

NOTHING TO DO?! YOU COULD READ A BOOK! OR WRITE A LETTER! OR TAKE A WALK!

WHEN YOU'RE OLD, YOU'LL WISH YOU HAD MORE THAN MEMORIES OF THIS TRIPE TO LOOK BACK ON.

UNDOUBTEDLY.

HI, DAD. IT'S ME, CALVIN!

HOW'S WORK GOING? ...UH HUH... PRETTY DAY OUT, ISN'T IT? ... YEP.....

ARE YOU BRINGING ME HOME ANY PRESENTS TONIGHT? ... NO? WELL, JUST THOUGHT I'D ASK...

LISTEN, I SUPPOSE YOU'RE WONDERING WHY I CALLED...

DAD, YOUR POLLS TOOK A BIG DIVE THIS WEEK.

YOUR "OVERALL DAD PERFORMANCE" RATING WAS ESPECIALLY LOW.

SEE? RIGHT ABOUT YESTERDAY YOUR POPULARITY WENT DOWN THE TUBES.

CALVIN, YOU DIDN'T GET DESSERT YESTERDAY BECAUSE YOU FLOODED THE HOUSE!!

I'D SUGGEST A NEW LINE OF WORK, "DAD"...

THE GIANT SLIMY OCTOPUS OOZES ACROSS THE BEACH.

HIS HIDEOUS PRESENCE TERRORIZES THE SLEEPY WATERFRONT COMMUNITY.

WITH A SUCKER-COVERED TENTACLE, HE GRABS AN UNSUSPECTING TOURIST.

A MUFFLED SCREAM LINGERS IN THE SALTY AIR!

DID YOU WANT SOMETHING, CALVIN?

ACK ICK IG

39

41

43

HEY, CALVIN! ARE WE NEAR A SLAUGHTERHOUSE, OR DID YOU FORGET YOUR DEODORANT?!

DROP DEAD, SUSIE! YOU'RE SO UGLY, I HEAR YOUR MOM PUTS A BAG OVER YOUR HEAD BEFORE SHE KISSES YOU GOODNIGHT!!

IT'S SHAMELESS THE WAY WE FLIRT.

WHAT'S IT LIKE TO FALL IN LOVE?

WELL..., SAY THE OBJECT OF YOUR AFFECTION WALKS BY...

YEAH?

FIRST, YOUR HEART FALLS INTO YOUR STOMACH AND SPLASHES YOUR INNARDS.

ALL THE MOISTURE MAKES YOU SWEAT PROFUSELY.

THIS CONDENSATION SHORTS THE CIRCUITS TO YOUR BRAIN, AND YOU GET ALL WOOZY.

WHEN YOUR BRAIN BURNS OUT ALTOGETHER, YOUR MOUTH DISENGAGES AND YOU BABBLE LIKE A CRETIN UNTIL SHE LEAVES.

THAT'S LOVE?!?

MEDICALLY SPEAKING.

HECK, THAT HAPPENED TO ME ONCE, BUT I FIGURED IT WAS COOTIES!!

WATTERSON

Hey, Calvin, it's gonna cost you 50 cents to be my friend today.

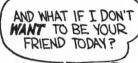

AND WHAT IF I DON'T *WANT* TO BE YOUR FRIEND TODAY?

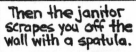

Then the janitor scrapes you off the wall with a spatula.

HECK, WHAT'S A LITTLE EXTORTION AMONG FRIENDS?

I GOT THE NEW ALBUM BY SCRAMBLED DEBUTANTE.

ALL THEIR SONGS GLORIFY DEPRAVED VIOLENCE, MINDLESS SEX, AND THE DELIBERATE ABUSE OF DANGEROUS DRUGS.

YOUR MOM'S GOING TO GO INTO CONNIPTIONS WHEN SHE SEES *THIS* LYING AROUND.

WELL I SURE DIDN'T BUY IT FOR THE MUSIC...

MOM, WILL YOU DRIVE ME INTO TOWN?

WHY SHOULD I *DRIVE* YOU, CALVIN? IT'S A PERFECT DAY OUTSIDE!

WHAT DO YOU THINK PEOPLE HAVE *FEET* FOR?

TO WORK THE GAS PEDAL.

I NEED HELP ON MY HOMEWORK. WHAT'S A PRONOUN?

A NOUN THAT LOST ITS AMATEUR STATUS.

MAYBE I CAN GET A POINT FOR ORIGINALITY.

LEAVE YOUR TIGER IN THE CAR, CALVIN.

CAN'T HOBBES COME ALONG, DAD? HE WON'T EAT ANYBODY!

NO, CALVIN. LET'S GO.

WELL, AT LEAST LET ME OPEN THE WINDOW AND GIVE HIM SOME AIR.

SEE IF HE'LL LEAVE THE KEYS, TOO, SO I CAN LISTEN TO THE RADIO.

CALVIN, YOUR MOTHER AND I HAVE DECIDED TO GIVE YOU AN ALLOWANCE.

IT'S IMPORTANT THAT ONE LEARNS THE VALUE OF MONEY.

MONEY! HA HA HA! I'M RICH! I'M RICH! I CAN BUY OFF ANYONE! THE WORLD IS MINE!

POWER! FRIENDS! PRESTIGE!

I BLEW IT AGAIN, DEAR!

I CAN BUY IT ALL! I'M FREE! HA HA HA HA!

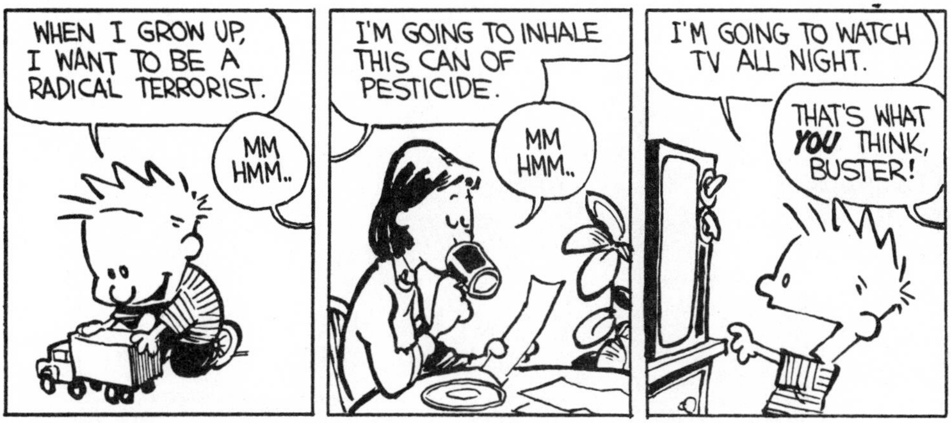
WHEN I GROW UP, I WANT TO BE A RADICAL TERRORIST.
MM HMM..
I'M GOING TO INHALE THIS CAN OF PESTICIDE.
MM HMM..
I'M GOING TO WATCH TV ALL NIGHT.
THAT'S WHAT **YOU** THINK, BUSTER!
YOU CAN NEVER TELL IF THEY'RE LISTENING OR NOT.

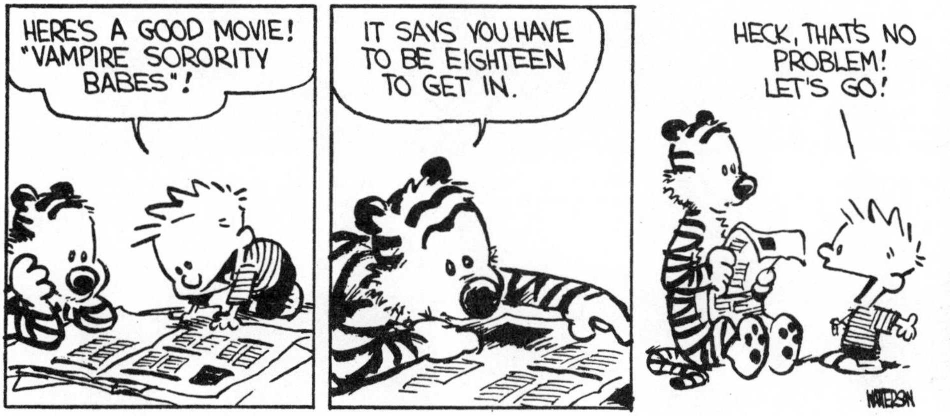
HERE'S A GOOD MOVIE! "VAMPIRE SORORITY BABES"!
IT SAYS YOU HAVE TO BE EIGHTEEN TO GET IN.
HECK, THAT'S NO PROBLEM! LET'S GO!
THIS IS A NEW ONE.
TWO PLEASE. ...I MEAN, ONE.

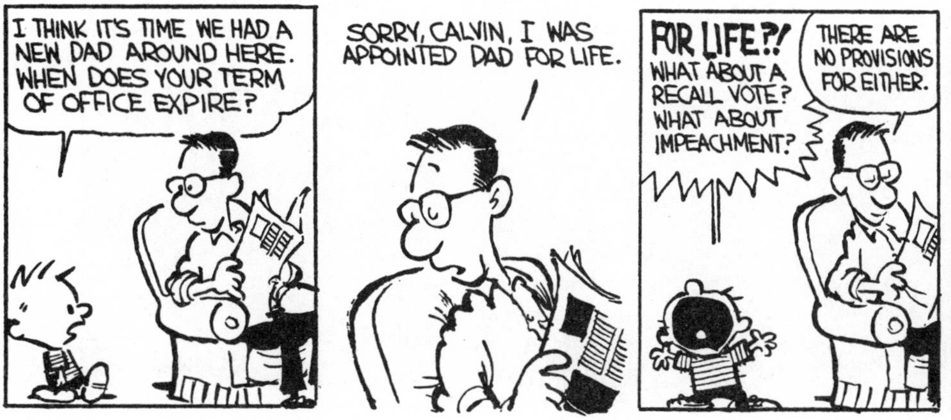
I THINK IT'S TIME WE HAD A NEW DAD AROUND HERE. WHEN DOES YOUR TERM OF OFFICE EXPIRE?
SORRY, CALVIN, I WAS APPOINTED DAD FOR LIFE.
FOR LIFE?! WHAT ABOUT A RECALL VOTE? WHAT ABOUT IMPEACHMENT?
THERE ARE NO PROVISIONS FOR EITHER.
DID YOU WRITE THIS CONSTITUTION YOURSELF, OR WHAT?
WELL, YOUR MOM HELPED SOME, TOO.

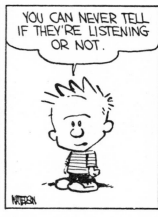

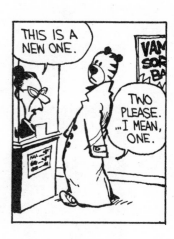

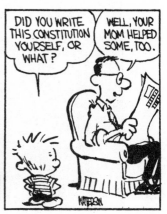

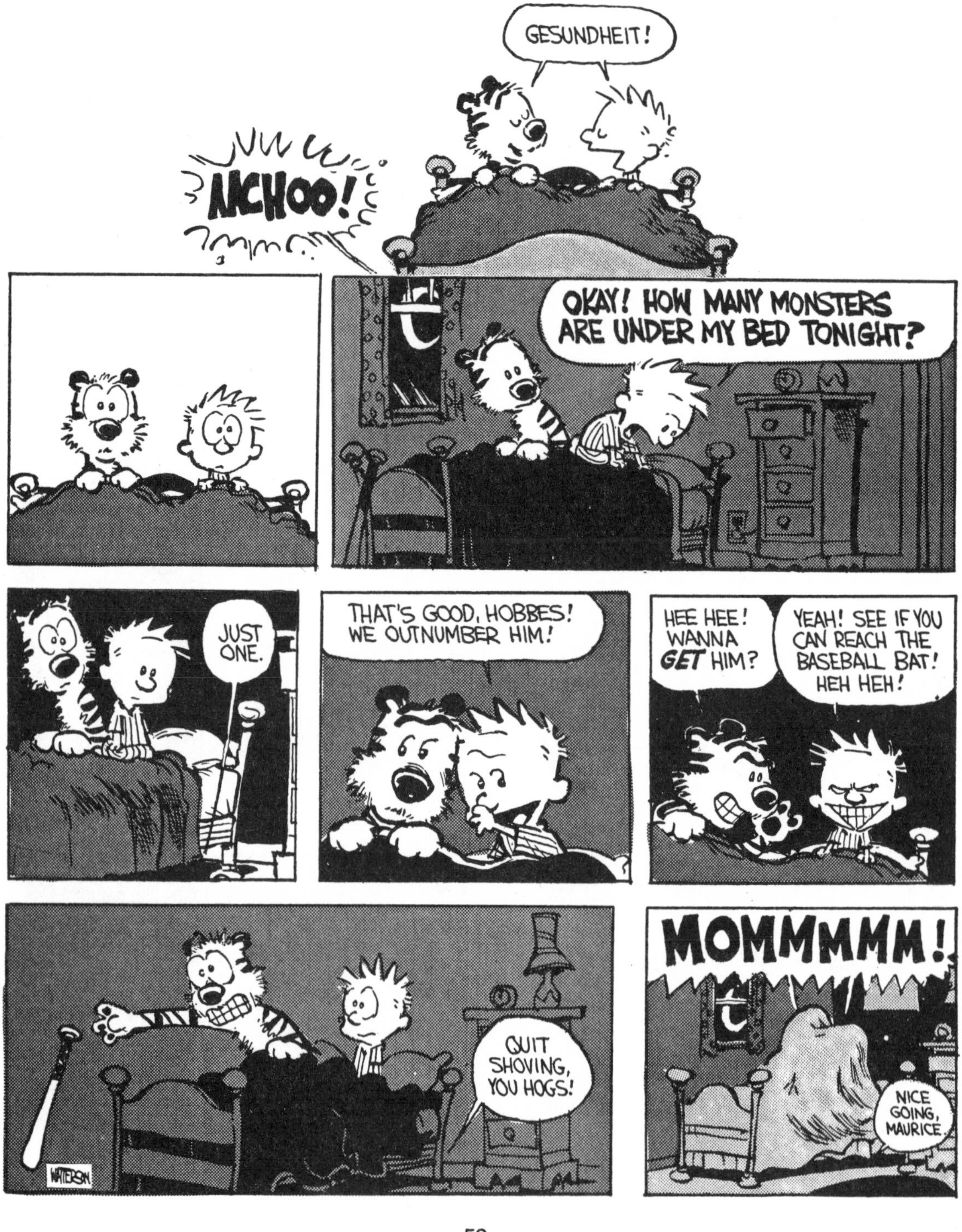

AACHOO!
GESUNDHEIT!
OKAY! HOW MANY MONSTERS ARE UNDER MY BED TONIGHT?
JUST ONE.
THAT'S GOOD, HOBBES! WE OUTNUMBER HIM!
HEE HEE! WANNA GET HIM?
YEAH! SEE IF YOU CAN REACH THE BASEBALL BAT! HEH HEH!
QUIT SHOVING, YOU HOGS!
WATTERSON
MOMMMMM!
NICE GOING, MAURICE.

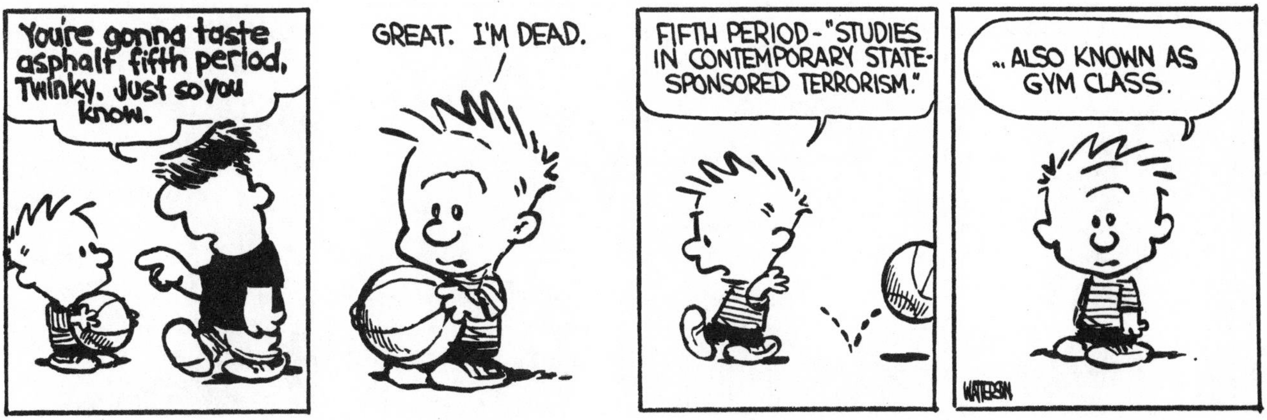
You're gonna taste asphalt fifth period, Twinky. Just so you know.
GREAT. I'M DEAD.
FIFTH PERIOD - "STUDIES IN CONTEMPORARY STATE-SPONSORED TERRORISM."
... ALSO KNOWN AS GYM CLASS.

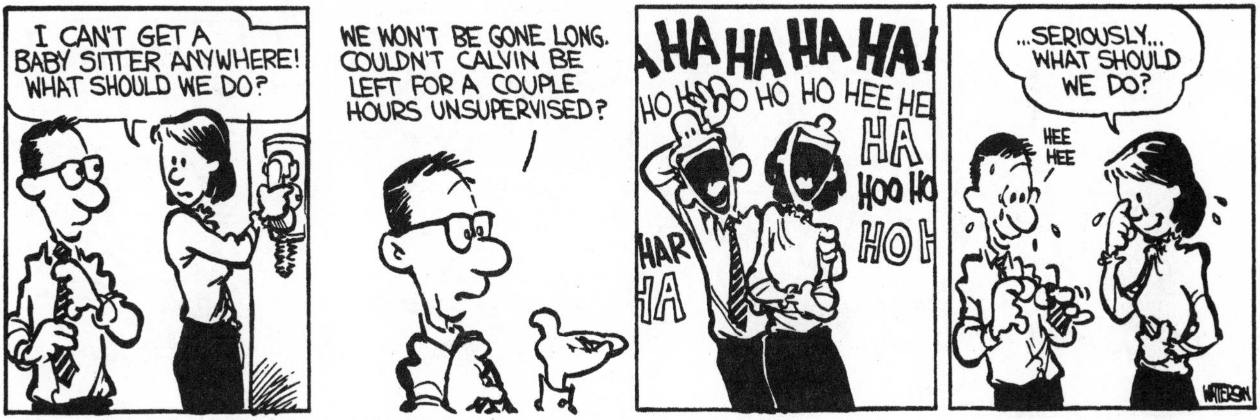
I CAN'T GET A BABY SITTER ANYWHERE! WHAT SHOULD WE DO?
WE WON'T BE GONE LONG. COULDN'T CALVIN BE LEFT FOR A COUPLE HOURS UNSUPERVISED?
HA HA HA HA HA
HO HO HO HO HO HEE HE
HA
HOO HO
HO H
HAR
HA
...SERIOUSLY... WHAT SHOULD WE DO?
HEE HEE

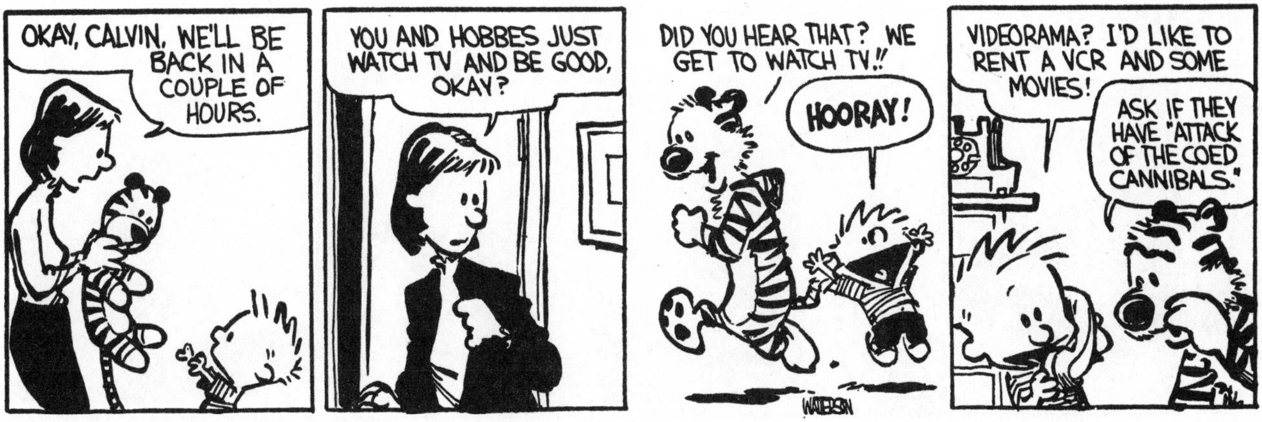
OKAY, CALVIN, WE'LL BE BACK IN A COUPLE OF HOURS.
YOU AND HOBBES JUST WATCH TV AND BE GOOD, OKAY?
DID YOU HEAR THAT? WE GET TO WATCH TV!!
HOORAY!
VIDEORAMA? I'D LIKE TO RENT A VCR AND SOME MOVIES!
ASK IF THEY HAVE "ATTACK OF THE COED CANNIBALS."

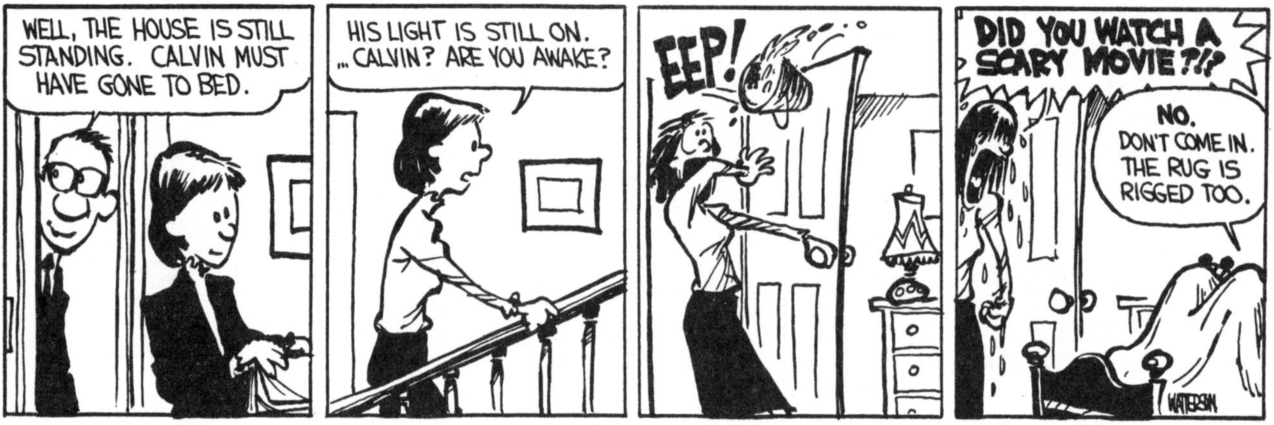
WELL, THE HOUSE IS STILL STANDING. CALVIN MUST HAVE GONE TO BED.
HIS LIGHT IS STILL ON. ... CALVIN? ARE YOU AWAKE?
EEP!
DID YOU WATCH A SCARY MOVIE?!?
NO. DON'T COME IN. THE RUG IS RIGGED TOO.
WATTERSON

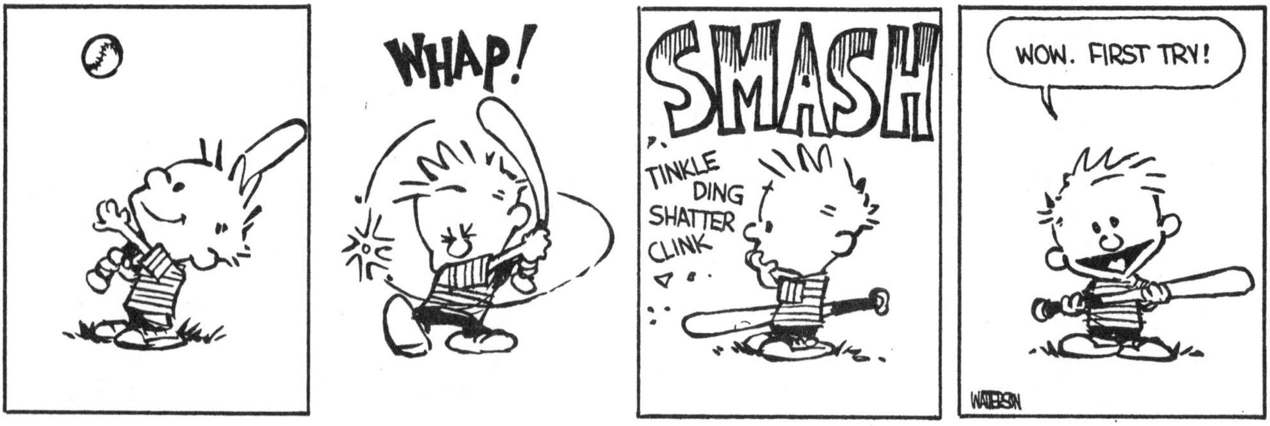
WHAP!
SMASH
TINKLE
DING
SHATTER
CLINK
WOW. FIRST TRY!
WATTERSON

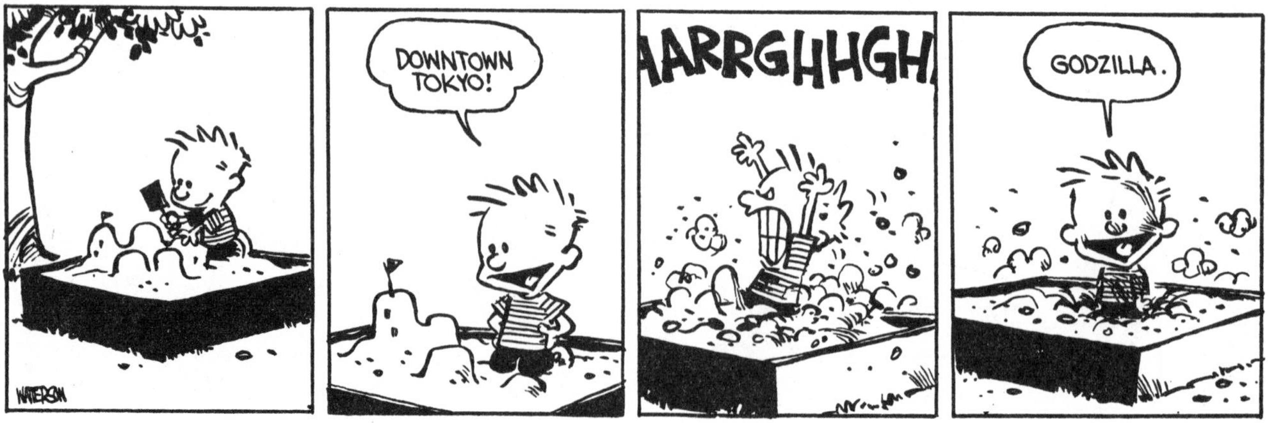
WATTERSON
DOWNTOWN TOKYO!
AARRGHHGH
GODZILLA.

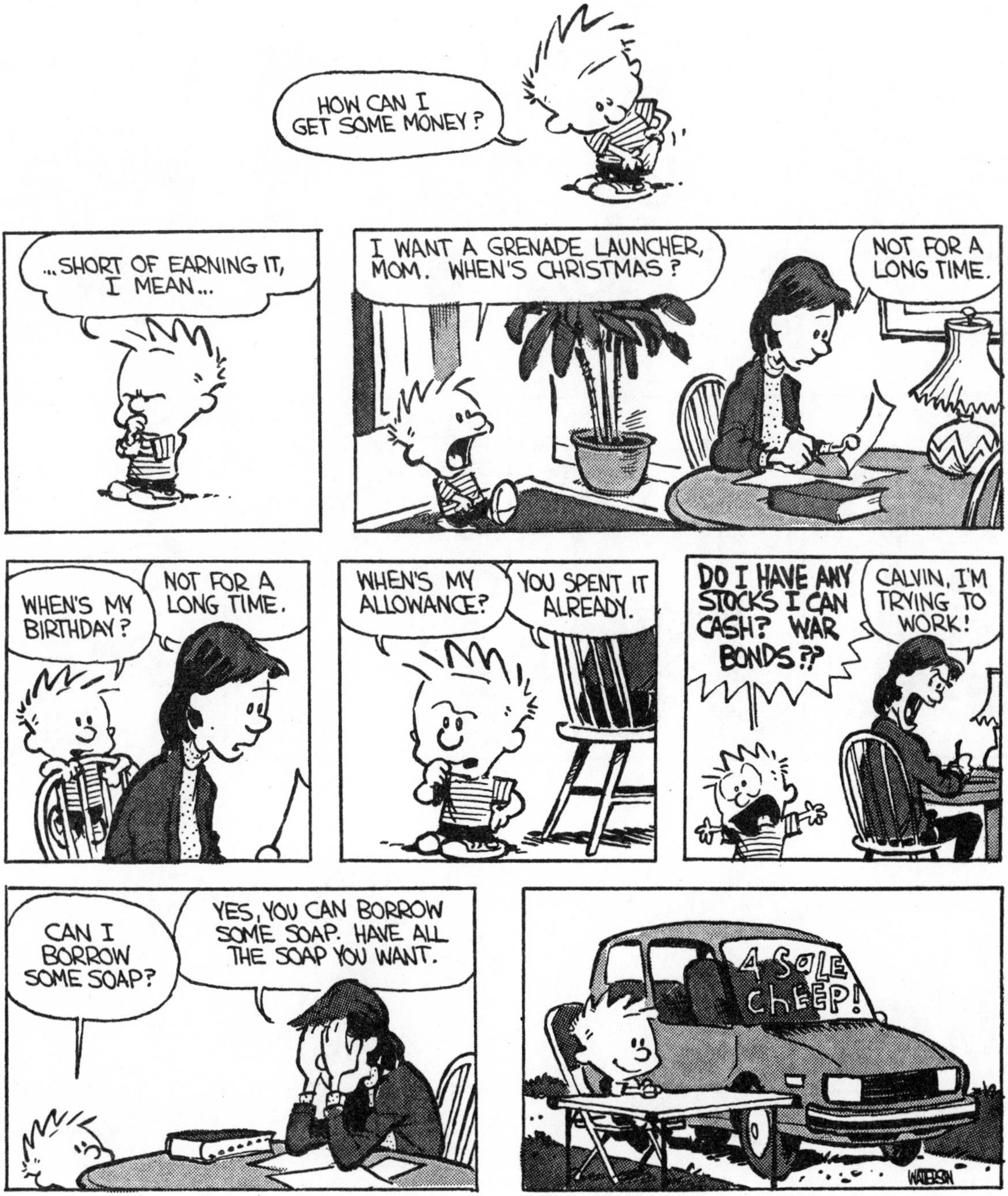
HOW CAN I GET SOME MONEY?
...SHORT OF EARNING IT, I MEAN...
I WANT A GRENADE LAUNCHER, MOM. WHEN'S CHRISTMAS?
NOT FOR A LONG TIME.
WHEN'S MY BIRTHDAY?
NOT FOR A LONG TIME.
WHEN'S MY ALLOWANCE?
YOU SPENT IT ALREADY.
DO I HAVE ANY STOCKS I CAN CASH? WAR BONDS?!?
CALVIN, I'M TRYING TO WORK!
CAN I BORROW SOME SOAP?
YES, YOU CAN BORROW SOME SOAP. HAVE ALL THE SOAP YOU WANT.
4 Sale CHEEP!
WATERSON

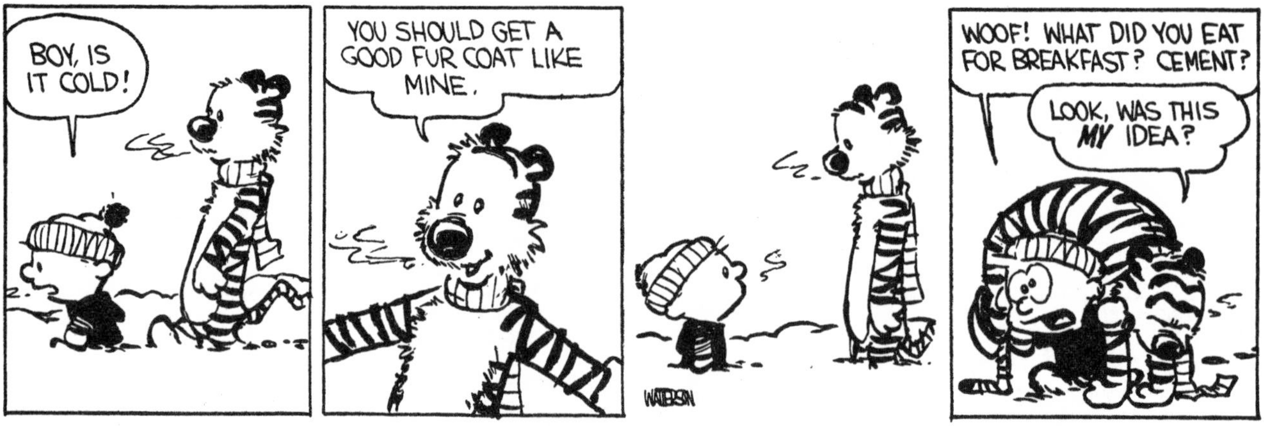
BOY, IS IT COLD!
YOU SHOULD GET A GOOD FUR COAT LIKE MINE.
WOOF! WHAT DID YOU EAT FOR BREAKFAST? CEMENT?
LOOK, WAS THIS *MY* IDEA?

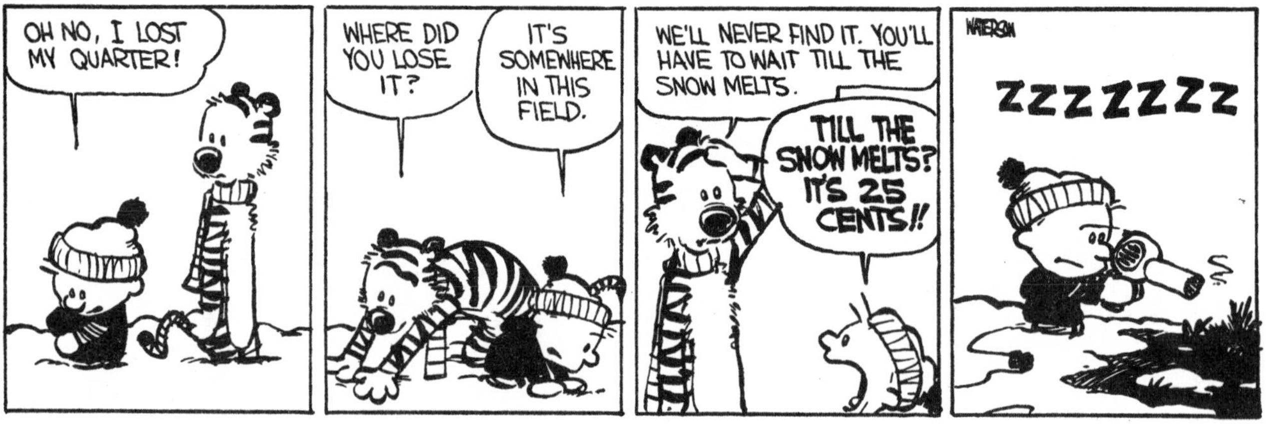
OH NO, I LOST MY QUARTER!
WHERE DID YOU LOSE IT?
IT'S SOMEWHERE IN THIS FIELD.
WE'LL NEVER FIND IT. YOU'LL HAVE TO WAIT TILL THE SNOW MELTS.
TILL THE SNOW MELTS? IT'S 25 CENTS!!
ZZZZZZZ

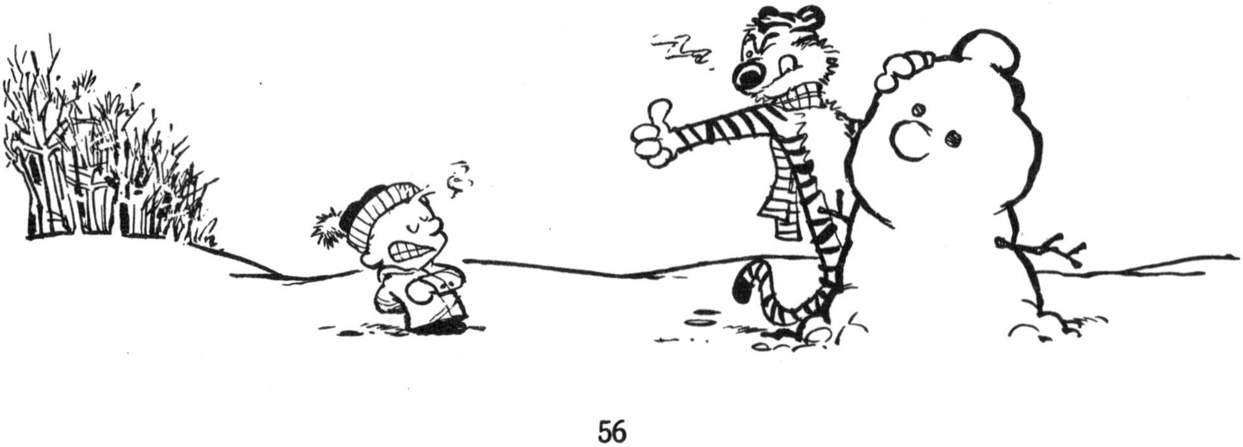

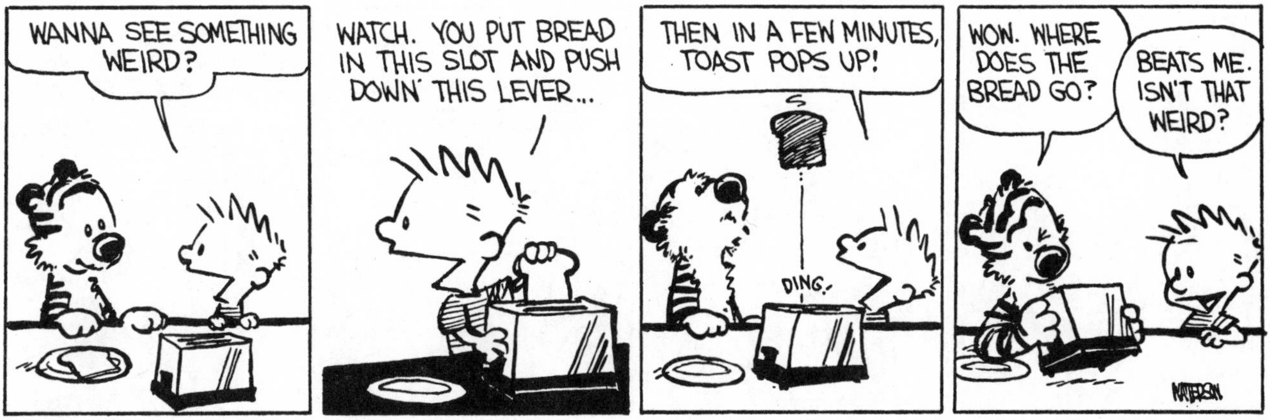
WANNA SEE SOMETHING WEIRD?
WATCH. YOU PUT BREAD IN THIS SLOT AND PUSH DOWN THIS LEVER...
THEN IN A FEW MINUTES, TOAST POPS UP!
DING!
WOW. WHERE DOES THE BREAD GO?
BEATS ME. ISN'T THAT WEIRD?

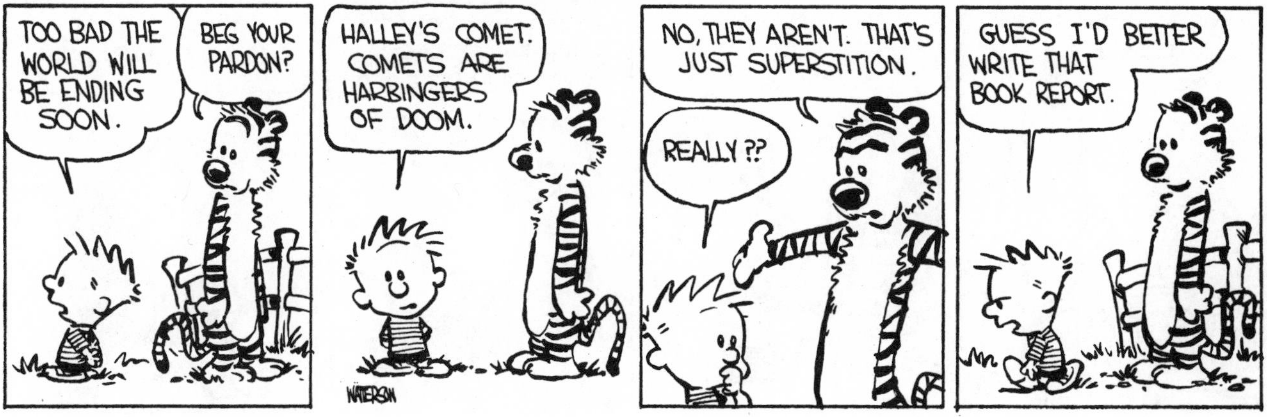
TOO BAD THE WORLD WILL BE ENDING SOON.
BEG YOUR PARDON?
HALLEY'S COMET. COMETS ARE HARBINGERS OF DOOM.
NO, THEY AREN'T. THAT'S JUST SUPERSTITION.
REALLY ??
GUESS I'D BETTER WRITE THAT BOOK REPORT.

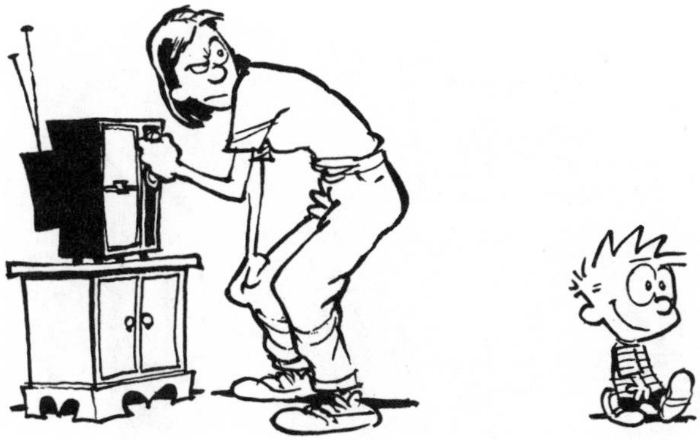

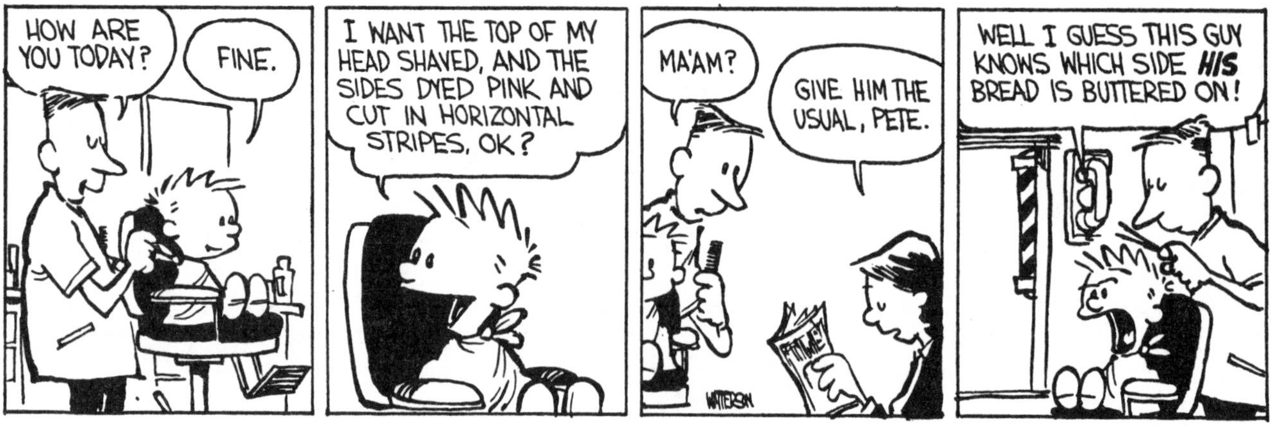
HOW ARE YOU TODAY?
FINE.
I WANT THE TOP OF MY HEAD SHAVED, AND THE SIDES DYED PINK AND CUT IN HORIZONTAL STRIPES, OK?
MA'AM?
GIVE HIM THE USUAL, PETE.
WELL I GUESS THIS GUY KNOWS WHICH SIDE ***HIS*** BREAD IS BUTTERED ON!

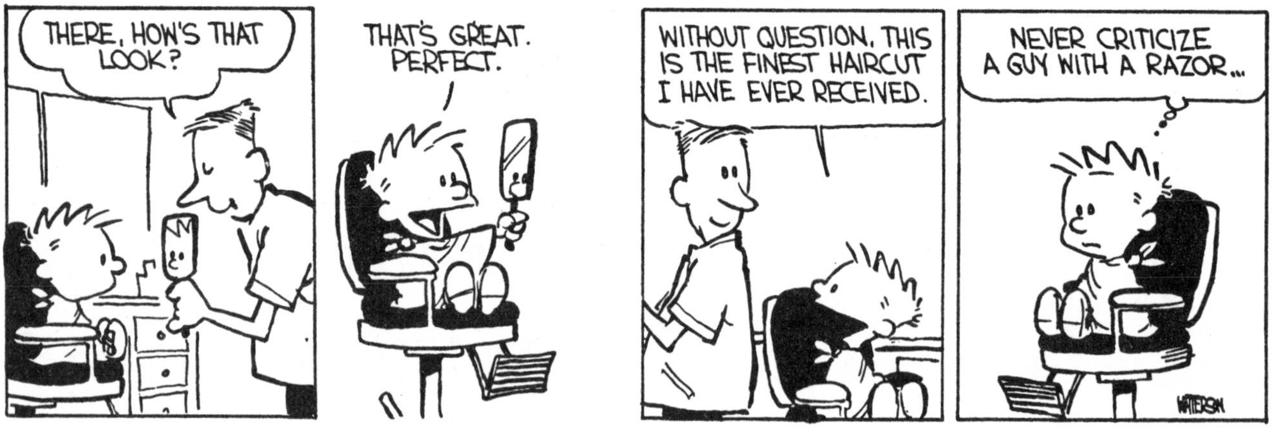
THERE, HOW'S THAT LOOK?
THAT'S GREAT. PERFECT.
WITHOUT QUESTION, THIS IS THE FINEST HAIRCUT I HAVE EVER RECEIVED.
NEVER CRITICIZE A GUY WITH A RAZOR...

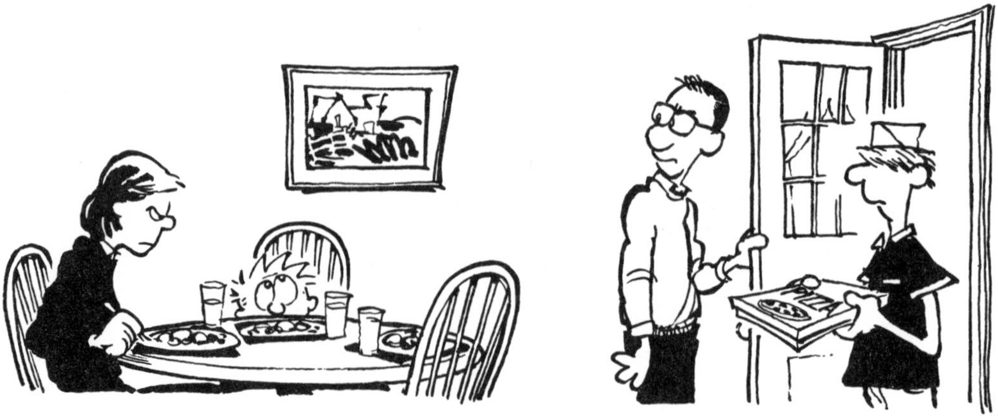

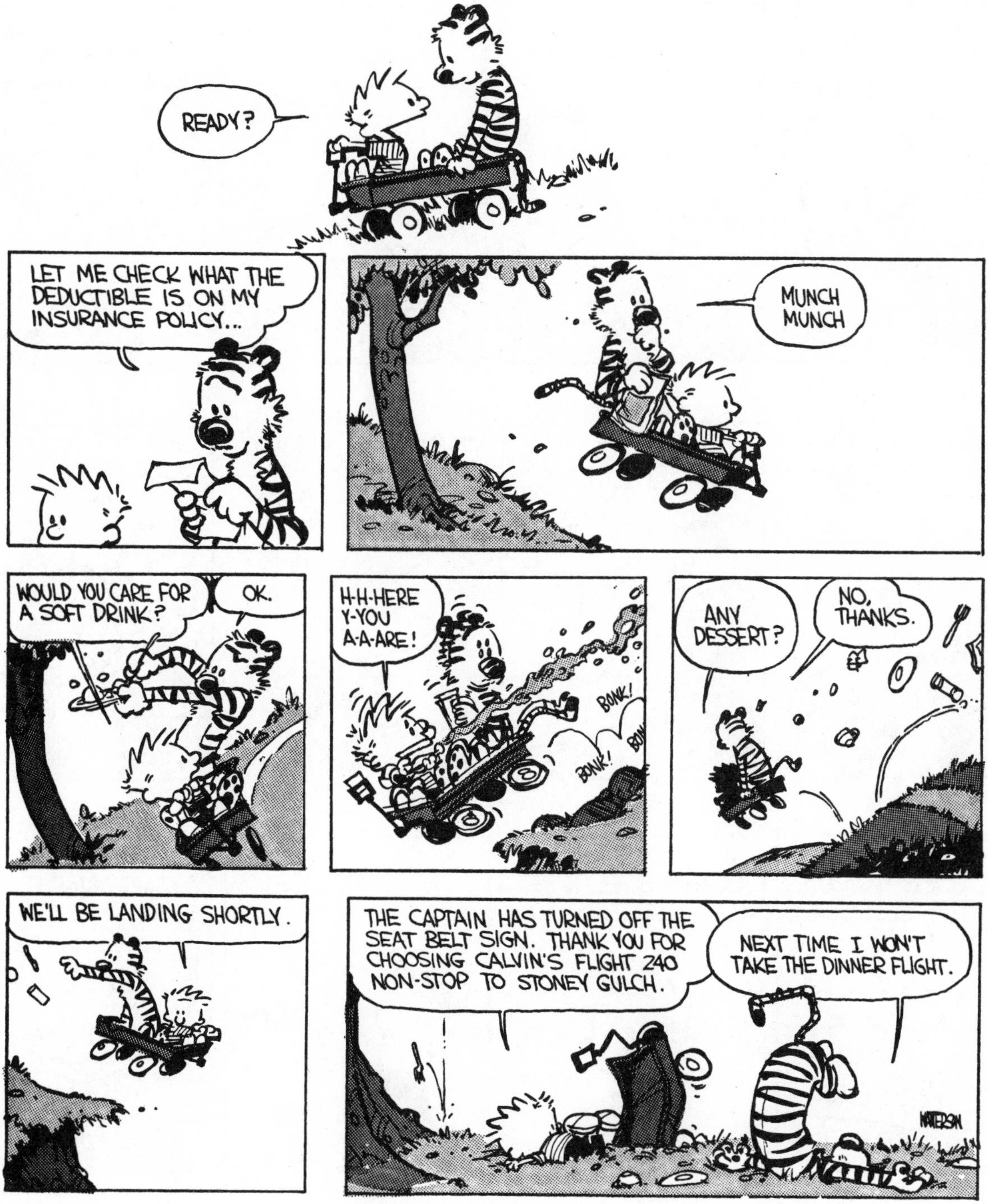
READY?
LET ME CHECK WHAT THE DEDUCTIBLE IS ON MY INSURANCE POLICY...
MUNCH MUNCH
WOULD YOU CARE FOR A SOFT DRINK?
OK.
H-H-HERE Y-YOU A-A-ARE!
BONK!
BONK!
ANY DESSERT?
NO, THANKS.
WE'LL BE LANDING SHORTLY.
THE CAPTAIN HAS TURNED OFF THE SEAT BELT SIGN. THANK YOU FOR CHOOSING CALVIN'S FLIGHT 240 NON-STOP TO STONEY GULCH.
NEXT TIME I WON'T TAKE THE DINNER FLIGHT.

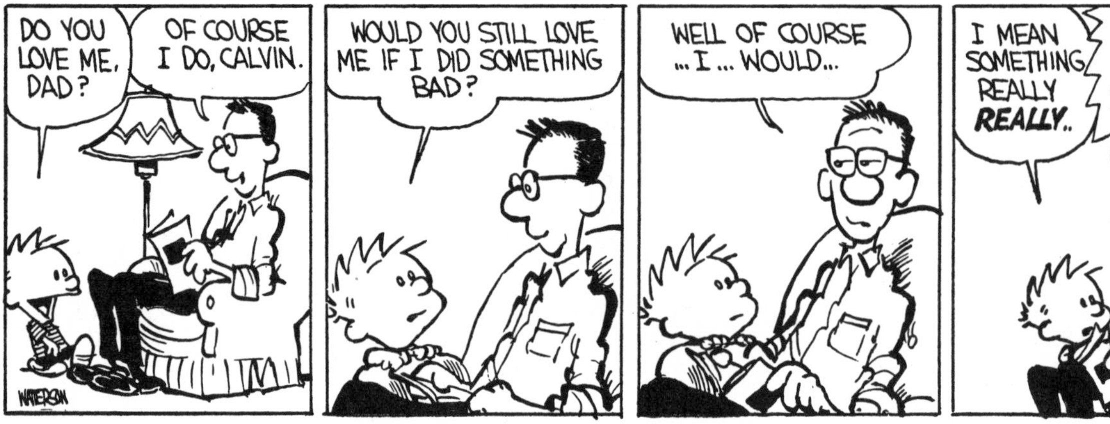
DO YOU LOVE ME, DAD?
OF COURSE I DO, CALVIN.
WOULD YOU STILL LOVE ME IF I DID SOMETHING BAD?
WELL OF COURSE ... I ... WOULD...
I MEAN SOMETHING REALLY *REALLY*..
CALVIN, WHAT DID YOU DO?!

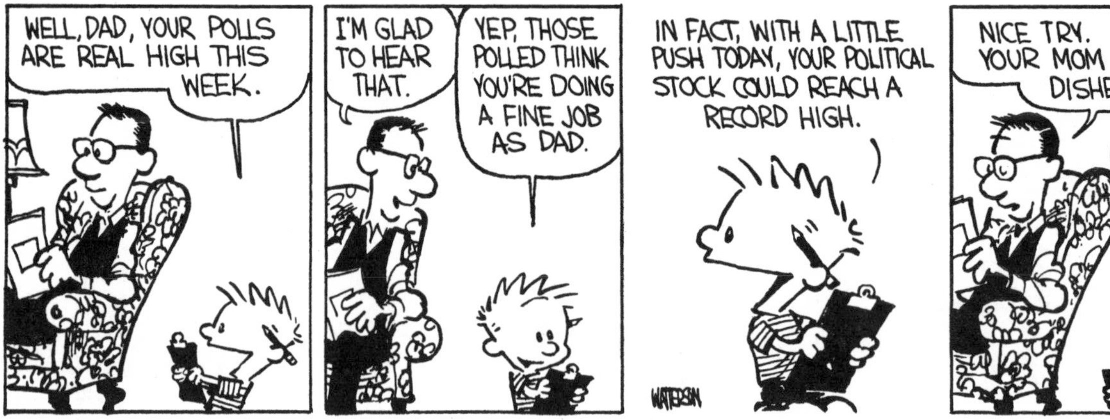
WELL, DAD, YOUR POLLS ARE REAL HIGH THIS WEEK.
I'M GLAD TO HEAR THAT.
YEP, THOSE POLLED THINK YOU'RE DOING A FINE JOB AS DAD.
IN FACT, WITH A LITTLE PUSH TODAY, YOUR POLITICAL STOCK COULD REACH A RECORD HIGH.
NICE TRY. GO HELP YOUR MOM WITH THE DISHES.
OOH DAD! SUICIDE! OOH! OOH!

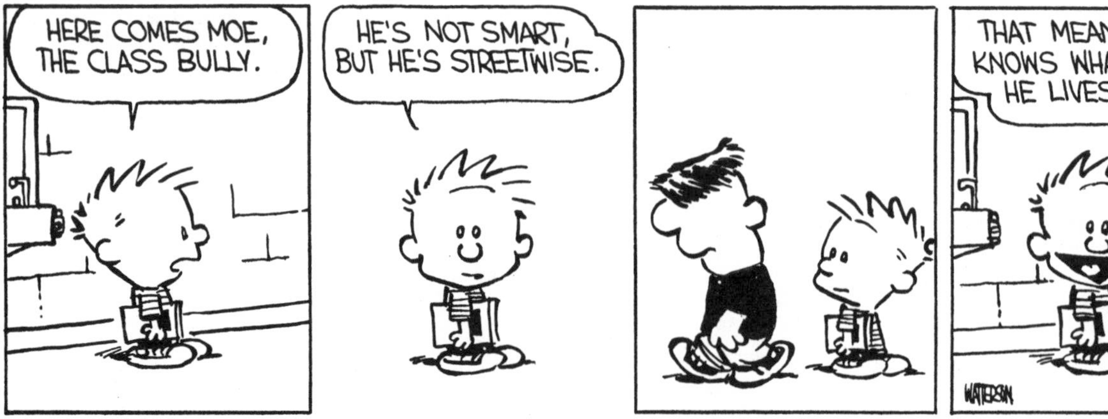
HERE COMES MOE, THE CLASS BULLY.
HE'S NOT SMART, BUT HE'S STREETWISE.
THAT MEANS HE KNOWS WHAT STREET HE LIVES ON.

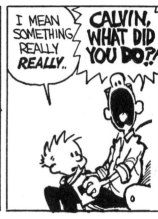

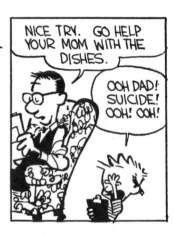

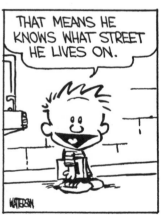

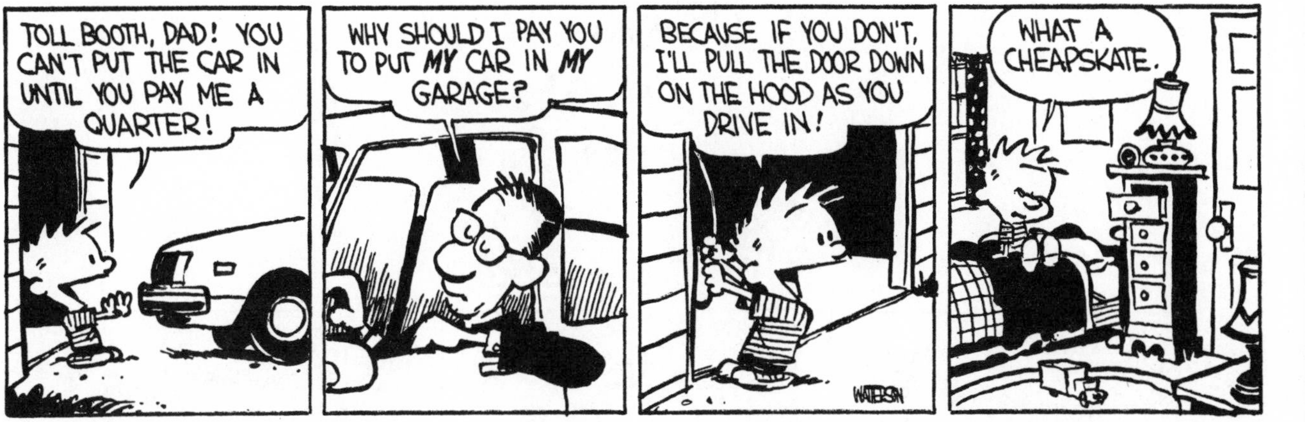
TOLL BOOTH, DAD! YOU CAN'T PUT THE CAR IN UNTIL YOU PAY ME A QUARTER!
WHY SHOULD I PAY YOU TO PUT *MY* CAR IN *MY* GARAGE?
BECAUSE IF YOU DON'T, I'LL PULL THE DOOR DOWN ON THE HOOD AS YOU DRIVE IN!
WHAT A CHEAPSKATE.

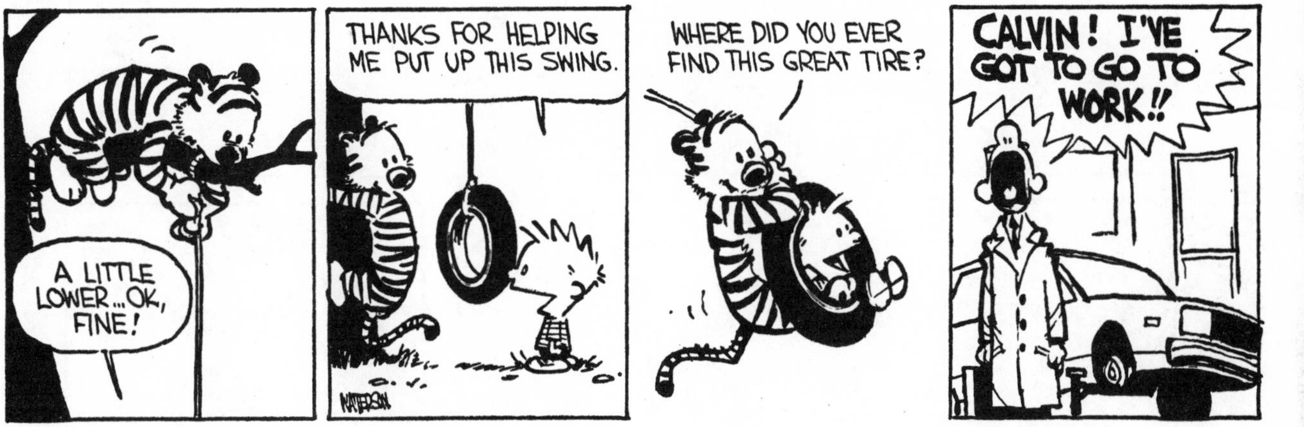
A LITTLE LOWER...OK, FINE!
THANKS FOR HELPING ME PUT UP THIS SWING.
WHERE DID YOU EVER FIND THIS GREAT TIRE?
CALVIN! I'VE GOT TO GO TO WORK!!

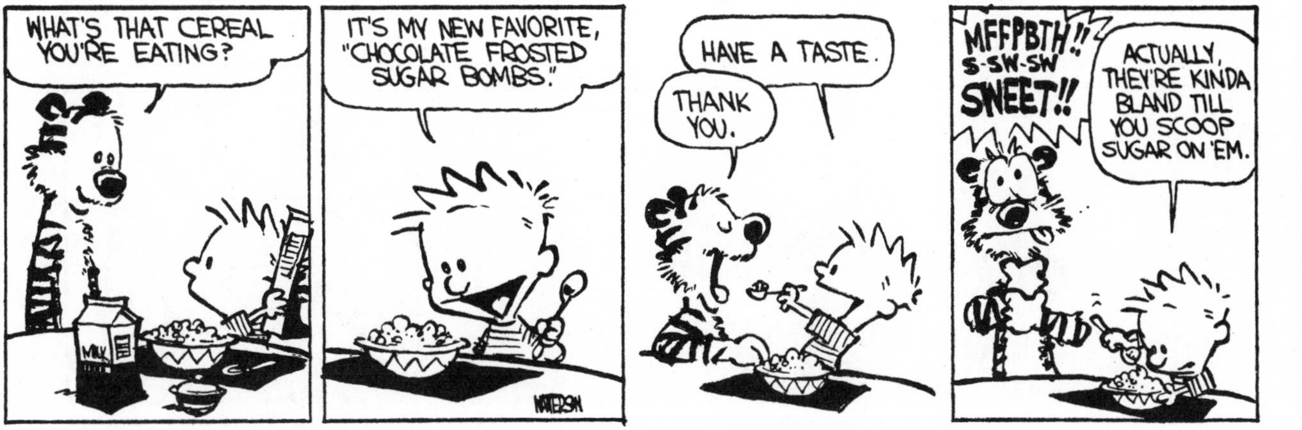
WHAT'S THAT CEREAL YOU'RE EATING?
IT'S MY NEW FAVORITE, "CHOCOLATE FROSTED SUGAR BOMBS."
HAVE A TASTE.
THANK YOU.
MFFPBTH!! S-SW-SW SWEET!!
ACTUALLY, THEY'RE KINDA BLAND TILL YOU SCOOP SUGAR ON 'EM.

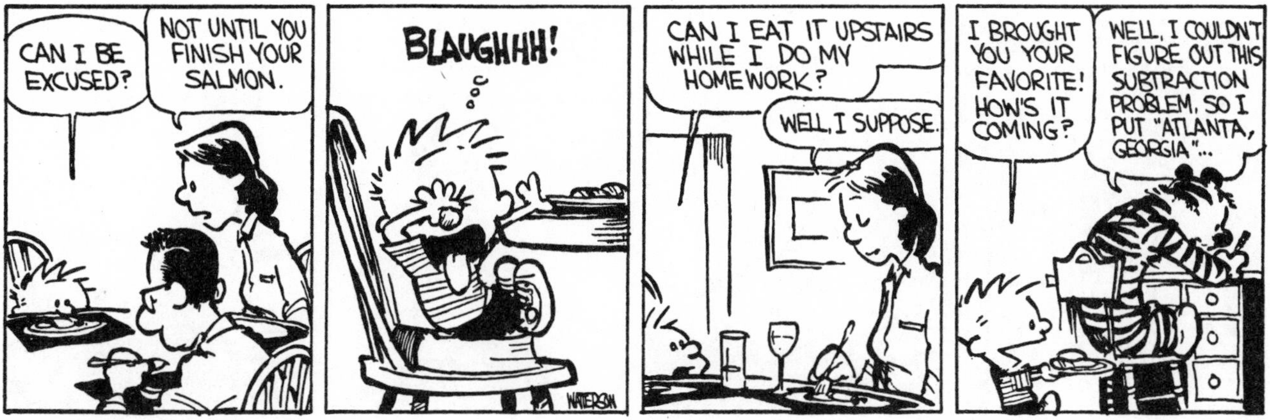
CAN I BE EXCUSED?
NOT UNTIL YOU FINISH YOUR SALMON.
BLAUGHHH!
CAN I EAT IT UPSTAIRS WHILE I DO MY HOMEWORK?
WELL, I SUPPOSE.
I BROUGHT YOU YOUR FAVORITE! HOW'S IT COMING?
WELL, I COULDN'T FIGURE OUT THIS SUBTRACTION PROBLEM, SO I PUT "ATLANTA, GEORGIA"...

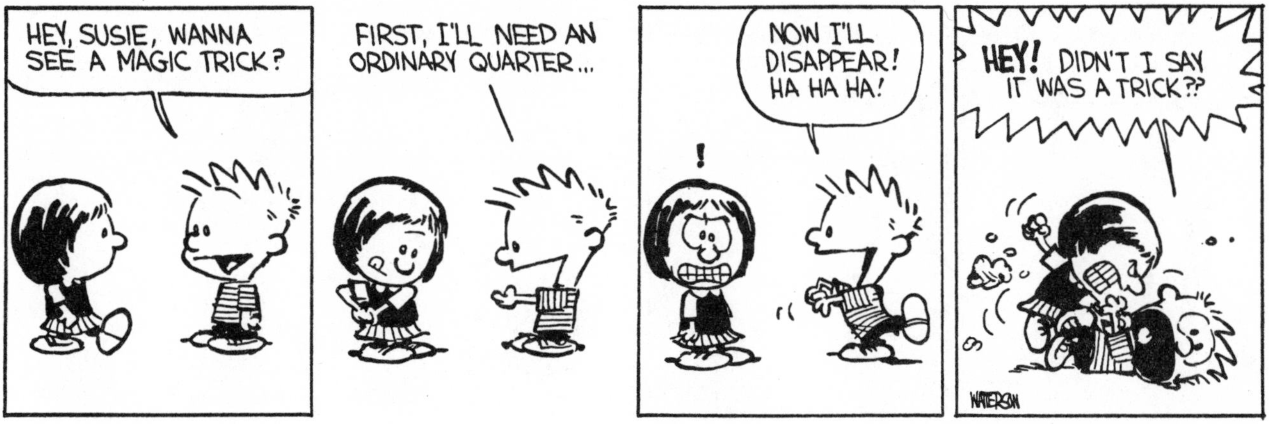
HEY, SUSIE, WANNA SEE A MAGIC TRICK?
FIRST, I'LL NEED AN ORDINARY QUARTER...
!
NOW I'LL DISAPPEAR! HA HA HA!
HEY! DIDN'T I SAY IT WAS A TRICK??

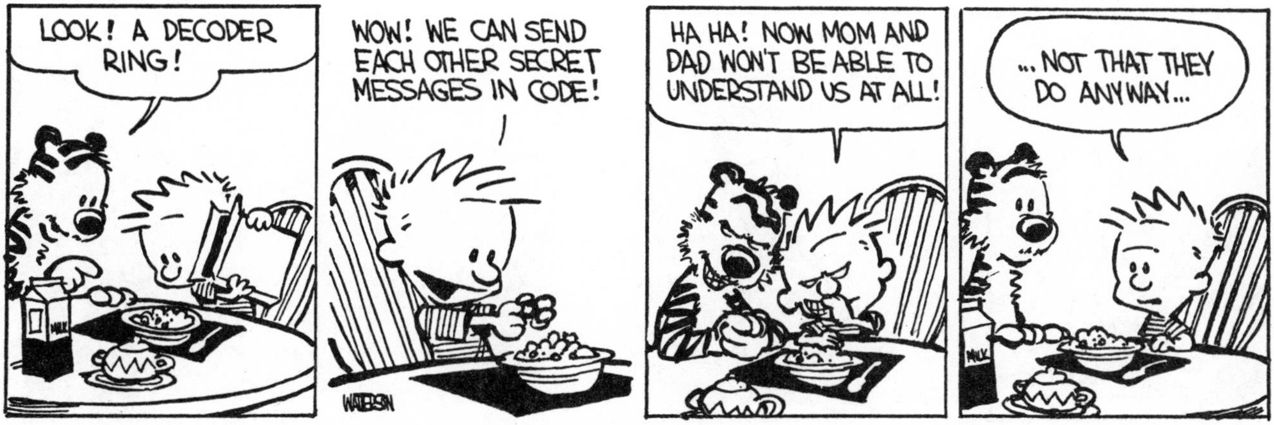
LOOK! A DECODER RING!
WOW! WE CAN SEND EACH OTHER SECRET MESSAGES IN CODE!
HA HA! NOW MOM AND DAD WON'T BE ABLE TO UNDERSTAND US AT ALL!
...NOT THAT THEY DO ANYWAY...

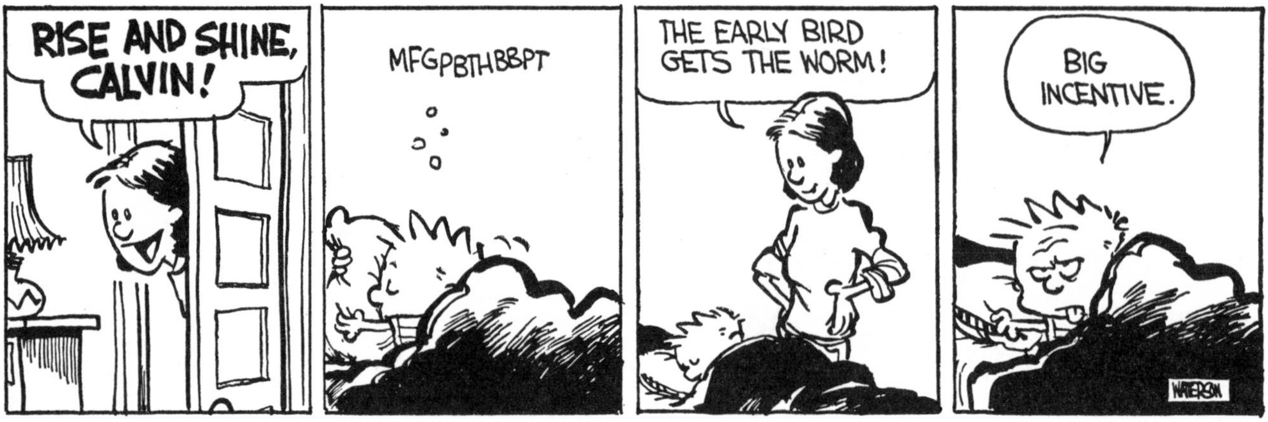
RISE AND SHINE, CALVIN!
MFGPBTHBBPT
THE EARLY BIRD GETS THE WORM!
BIG INCENTIVE.
WATTERSON

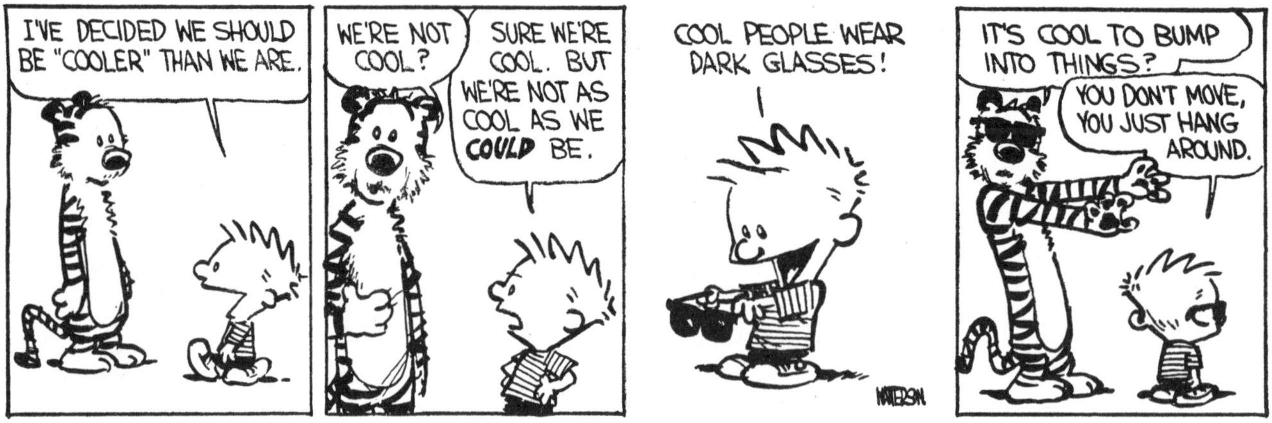
I'VE DECIDED WE SHOULD BE "COOLER" THAN WE ARE.
WE'RE NOT COOL?
SURE WE'RE COOL. BUT WE'RE NOT AS COOL AS WE **COULD** BE.
COOL PEOPLE WEAR DARK GLASSES!
WATTERSON
IT'S COOL TO BUMP INTO THINGS?
YOU DON'T MOVE, YOU JUST HANG AROUND.

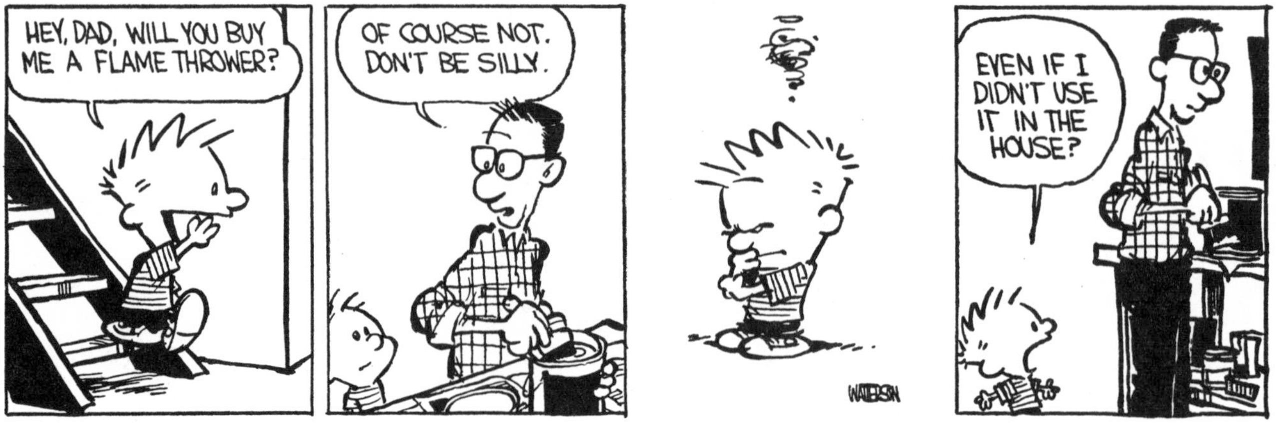
HEY, DAD, WILL YOU BUY ME A FLAME THROWER?
OF COURSE NOT. DON'T BE SILLY.
WATTERSON
EVEN IF I DIDN'T USE IT IN THE HOUSE?

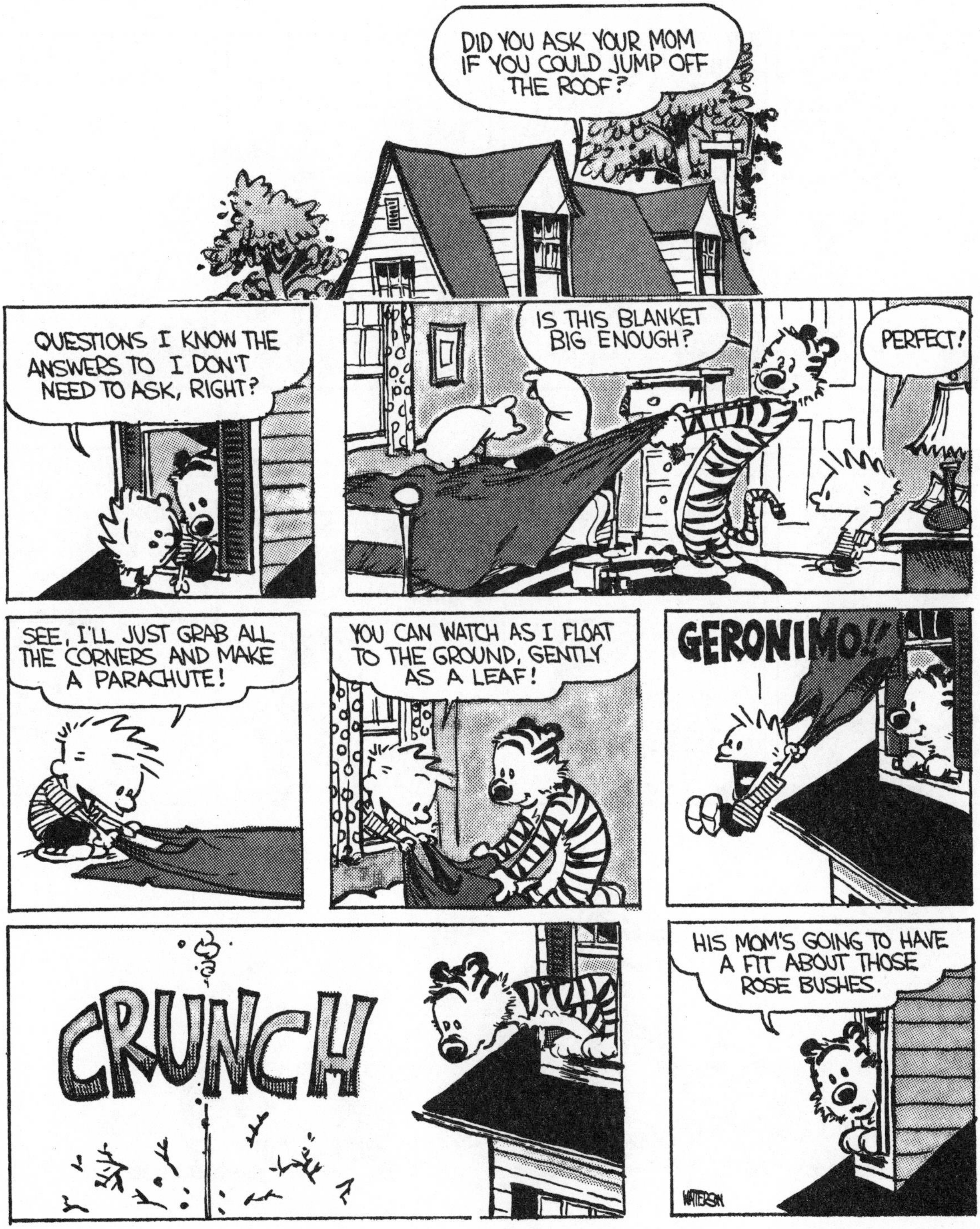
DID YOU ASK YOUR MOM IF YOU COULD JUMP OFF THE ROOF?
QUESTIONS I KNOW THE ANSWERS TO I DON'T NEED TO ASK, RIGHT?
IS THIS BLANKET BIG ENOUGH?
PERFECT!
SEE, I'LL JUST GRAB ALL THE CORNERS AND MAKE A PARACHUTE!
YOU CAN WATCH AS I FLOAT TO THE GROUND, GENTLY AS A LEAF!
GERONIMO!!
CRUNCH
HIS MOM'S GOING TO HAVE A FIT ABOUT THOSE ROSE BUSHES.
WATTERSON

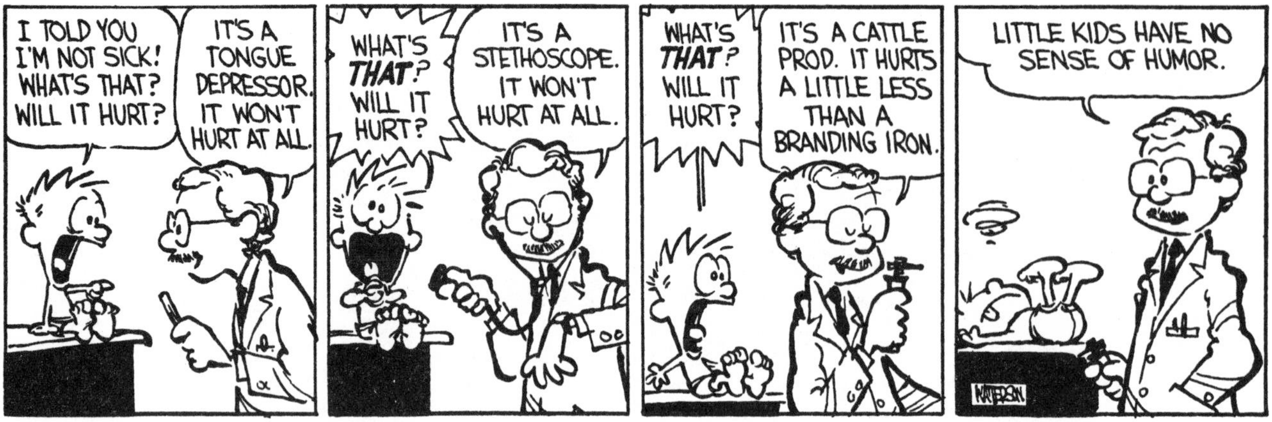
I TOLD YOU I'M NOT SICK! WHAT'S THAT? WILL IT HURT?
IT'S A TONGUE DEPRESSOR. IT WON'T HURT AT ALL.
WHAT'S THAT? WILL IT HURT?
IT'S A STETHOSCOPE. IT WON'T HURT AT ALL.
WHAT'S THAT? WILL IT HURT?
IT'S A CATTLE PROD. IT HURTS A LITTLE LESS THAN A BRANDING IRON.
LITTLE KIDS HAVE NO SENSE OF HUMOR.

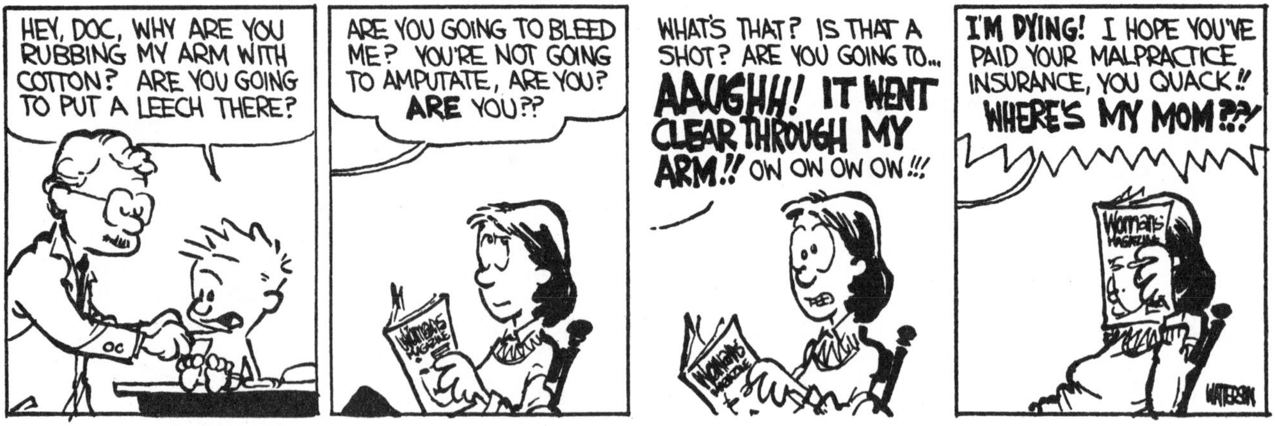
HEY, DOC, WHY ARE YOU RUBBING MY ARM WITH COTTON? ARE YOU GOING TO PUT A LEECH THERE?
ARE YOU GOING TO BLEED ME? YOU'RE NOT GOING TO AMPUTATE, ARE YOU? ARE YOU??
WHAT'S THAT? IS THAT A SHOT? ARE YOU GOING TO... AAUGHH! IT WENT CLEAR THROUGH MY ARM!! OW OW OW OW!!!
I'M DYING! I HOPE YOU'VE PAID YOUR MALPRACTICE INSURANCE, YOU QUACK!! WHERE'S MY MOM???

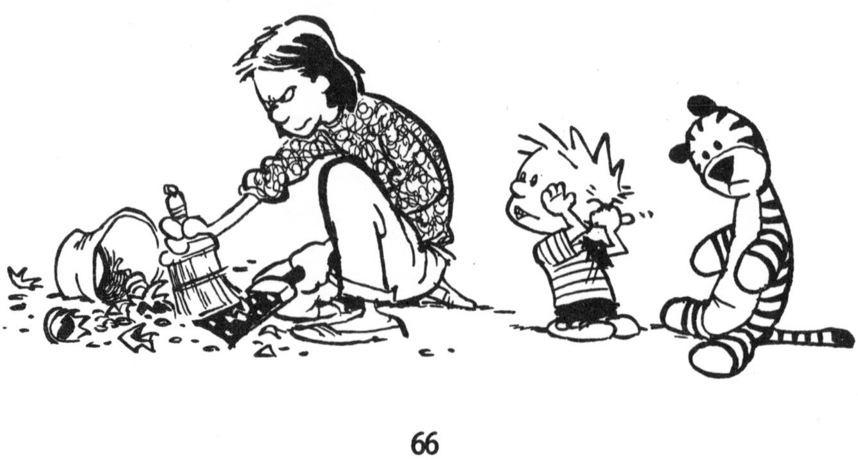

"SAFARI AL" HACKS HIS WAY THROUGH THE JUNGLE!

SUDDENLY, A GIANT GORILLA RIPS THROUGH THE FOLIAGE!

CLEAN YOUR ROOM.

WHAT?

YOU HEARD ME. IT'S A JUNGLE IN HERE!

SEEN ANY UFOs YET?

NOPE.

KEEP WATCHING THE MOON. ALIENS USUALLY TRY TO SNEAK UP FROM BEHIND IT.

WHAT ARE YOU DOING OUT HERE IN YOUR PAJAMAS? GET BACK IN BED!!

MOTHERS, ON THE OTHER HAND, SNEAK UP FROM BEHIND THE PACHYSANDRA PATCH.

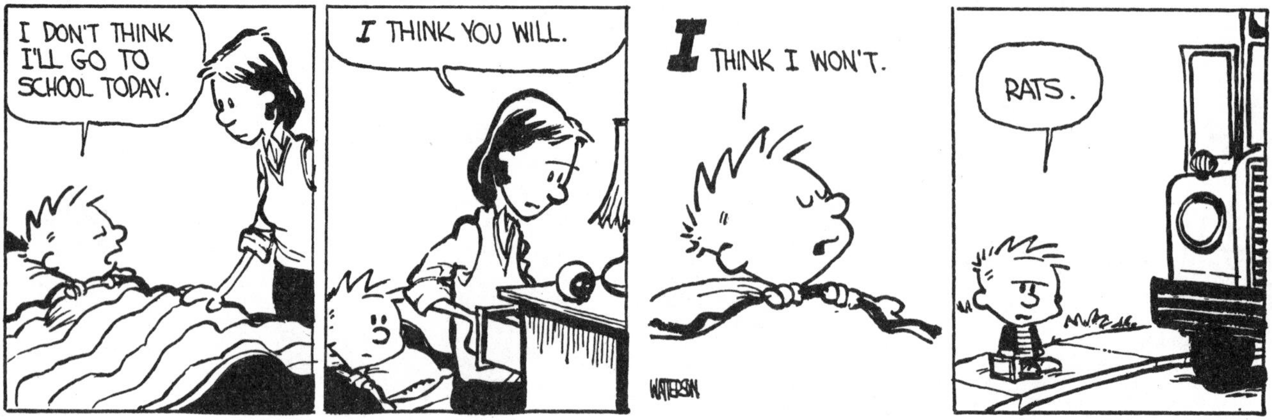
I DON'T THINK I'LL GO TO SCHOOL TODAY.
I THINK YOU WILL.
I THINK I WON'T.
WATERSON
RATS.

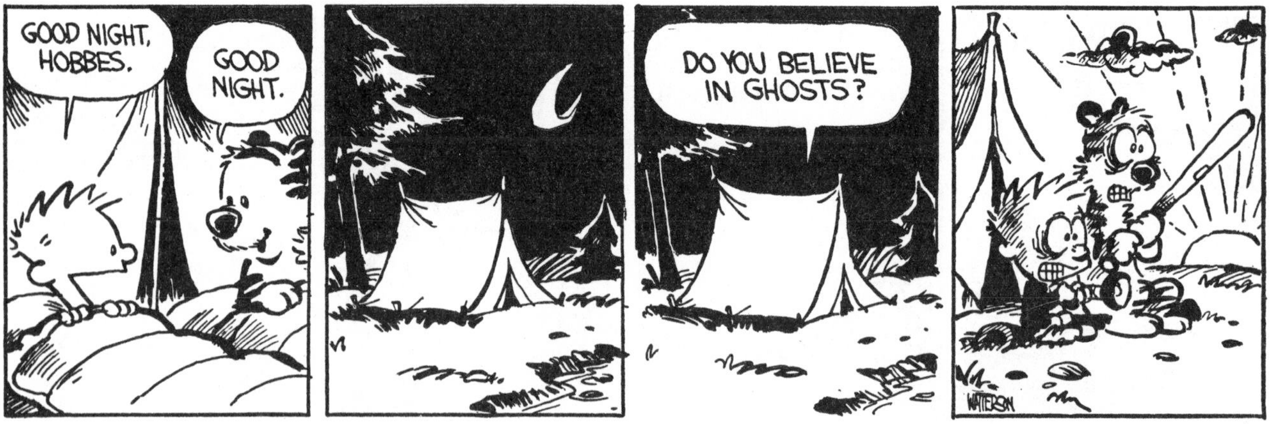
GOOD NIGHT, HOBBES.
GOOD NIGHT.
DO YOU BELIEVE IN GHOSTS?
WATERSON

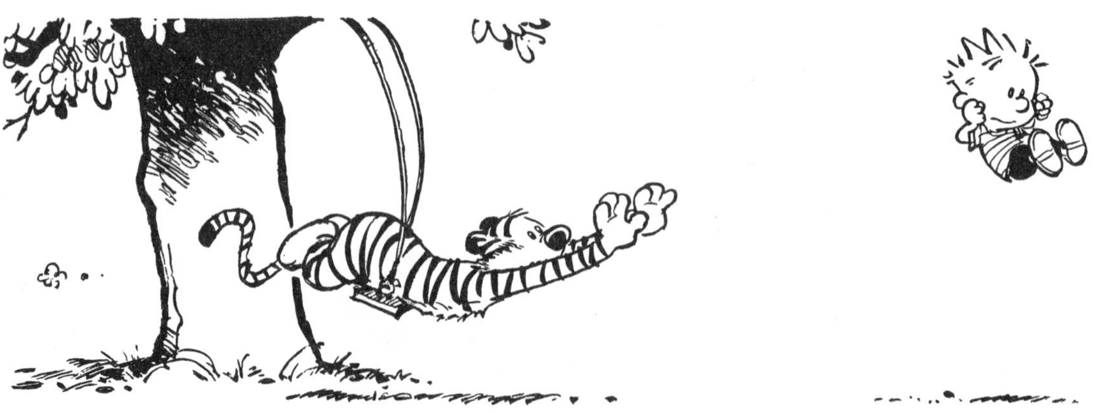

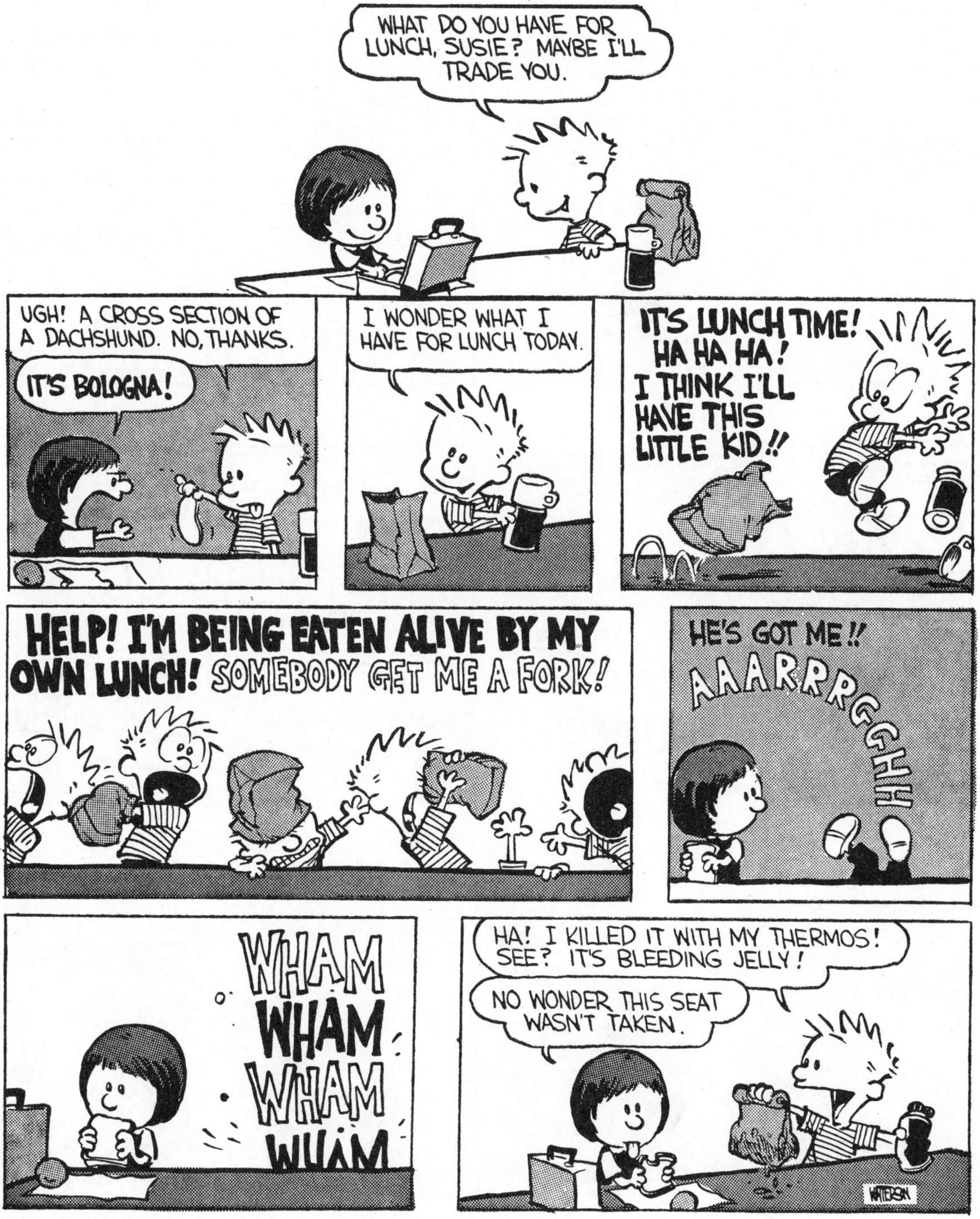
WHAT DO YOU HAVE FOR LUNCH, SUSIE? MAYBE I'LL TRADE YOU.
UGH! A CROSS SECTION OF A DACHSHUND. NO, THANKS.
IT'S BOLOGNA!
I WONDER WHAT I HAVE FOR LUNCH TODAY.
IT'S LUNCH TIME! HA HA HA! I THINK I'LL HAVE THIS LITTLE KID!!
HELP! I'M BEING EATEN ALIVE BY MY OWN LUNCH! SOMEBODY GET ME A FORK!
HE'S GOT ME!!
AAARRRGGHH
WHAM
WHAM
WHAM
WHAM
HA! I KILLED IT WITH MY THERMOS! SEE? IT'S BLEEDING JELLY!
NO WONDER THIS SEAT WASN'T TAKEN.
WATTERSON

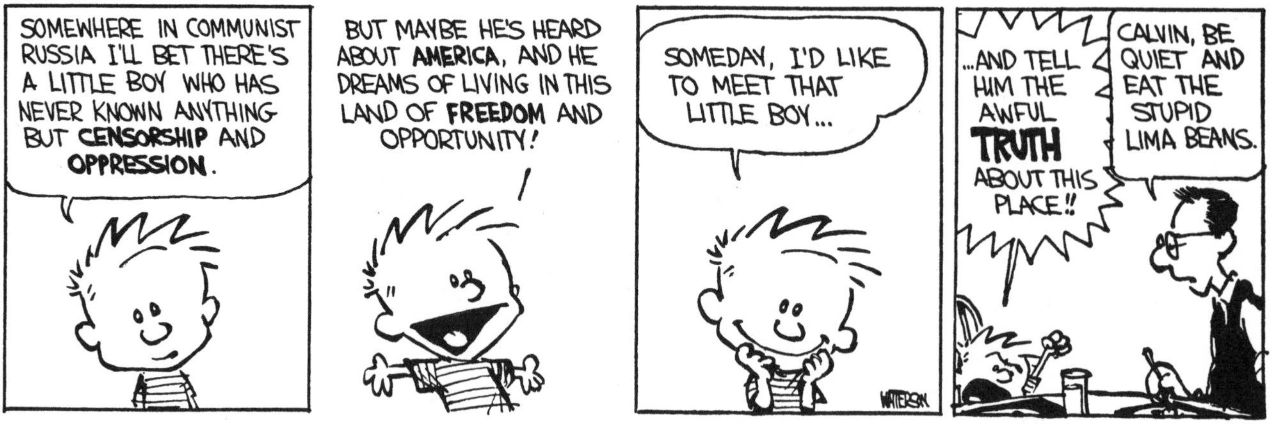
SOMEWHERE IN COMMUNIST RUSSIA I'LL BET THERE'S A LITTLE BOY WHO HAS NEVER KNOWN ANYTHING BUT CENSORSHIP AND OPPRESSION.
BUT MAYBE HE'S HEARD ABOUT AMERICA, AND HE DREAMS OF LIVING IN THIS LAND OF FREEDOM AND OPPORTUNITY!
SOMEDAY, I'D LIKE TO MEET THAT LITTLE BOY...
...AND TELL HIM THE AWFUL TRUTH ABOUT THIS PLACE!!
CALVIN, BE QUIET AND EAT THE STUPID LIMA BEANS.
WATTERSON

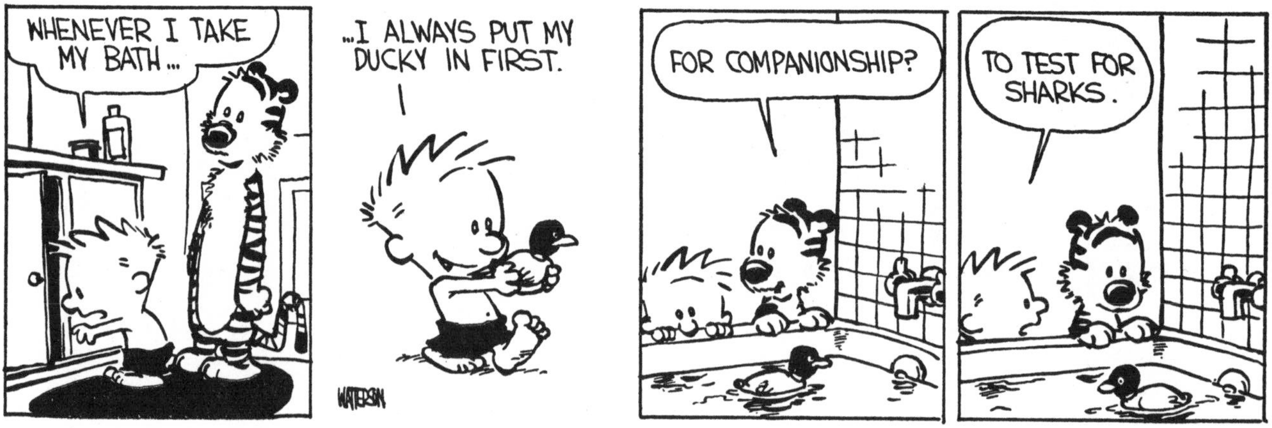
WHENEVER I TAKE MY BATH...
...I ALWAYS PUT MY DUCKY IN FIRST.
WATTERSON
FOR COMPANIONSHIP?
TO TEST FOR SHARKS.

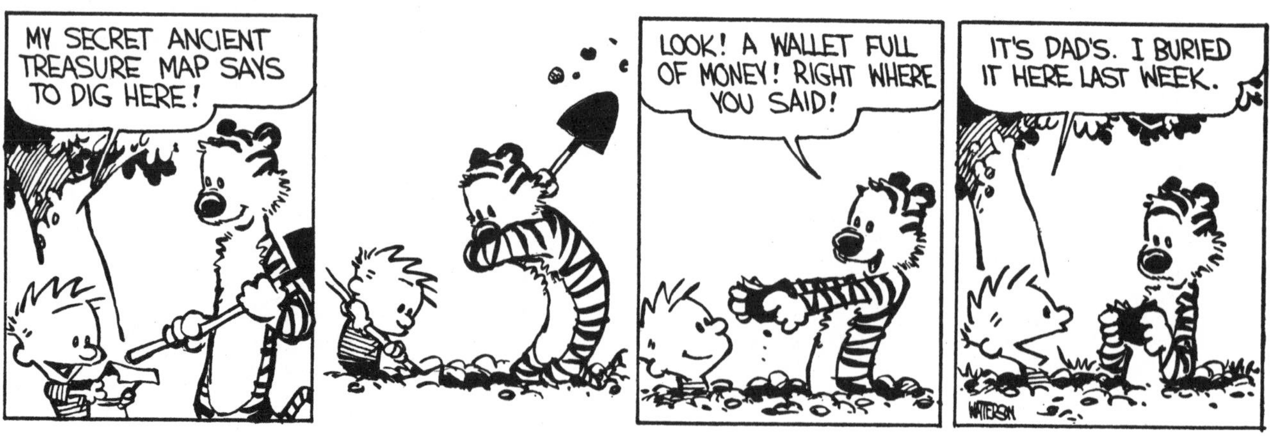
MY SECRET ANCIENT TREASURE MAP SAYS TO DIG HERE!
LOOK! A WALLET FULL OF MONEY! RIGHT WHERE YOU SAID!
IT'S DAD'S. I BURIED IT HERE LAST WEEK.
WATTERSON

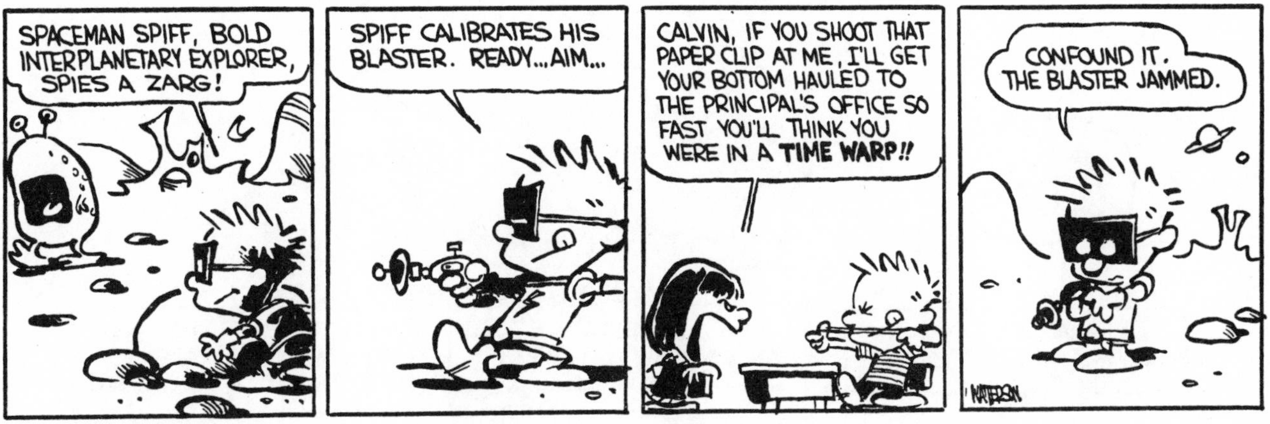
SPACEMAN SPIFF, BOLD INTERPLANETARY EXPLORER, SPIES A ZARG!
SPIFF CALIBRATES HIS BLASTER. READY...AIM...
CALVIN, IF YOU SHOOT THAT PAPER CLIP AT ME, I'LL GET YOUR BOTTOM HAULED TO THE PRINCIPAL'S OFFICE SO FAST YOU'LL THINK YOU WERE IN A **TIME WARP**!!
CONFOUND IT. THE BLASTER JAMMED.

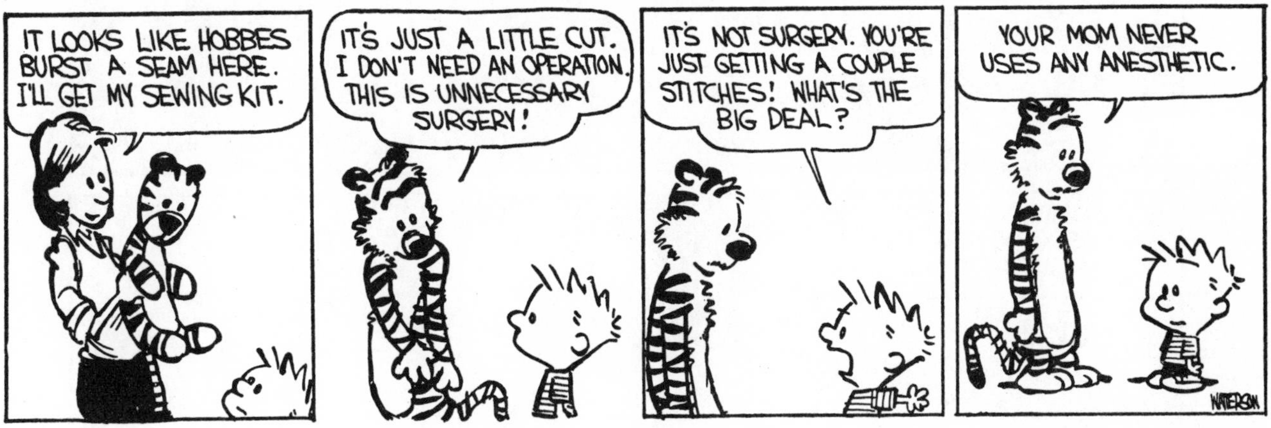
IT LOOKS LIKE HOBBES BURST A SEAM HERE. I'LL GET MY SEWING KIT.
IT'S JUST A LITTLE CUT. I DON'T NEED AN OPERATION. THIS IS UNNECESSARY SURGERY!
IT'S NOT SURGERY. YOU'RE JUST GETTING A COUPLE STITCHES! WHAT'S THE BIG DEAL?
YOUR MOM NEVER USES ANY ANESTHETIC.

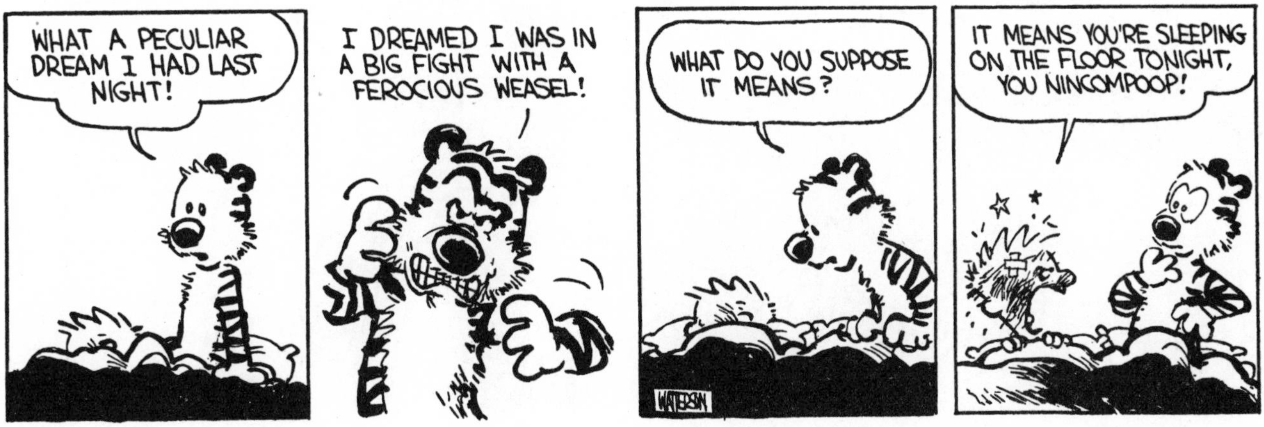
WHAT A PECULIAR DREAM I HAD LAST NIGHT!
I DREAMED I WAS IN A BIG FIGHT WITH A FEROCIOUS WEASEL!
WHAT DO YOU SUPPOSE IT MEANS?
IT MEANS YOU'RE SLEEPING ON THE FLOOR TONIGHT, YOU NINCOMPOOP!

WHY SURE.

HEY DAD, REMEMBER OUR CAR?

WAIT A MINUTE. WHAT DO YOU MEAN, "REMEMBER"?

HOBBES, I HAVE A CONJECTURAL MORAL QUESTION. MAYBE YOU CAN HELP.

SURE.

SUPPOSE I DID SOMETHING BAD. SHOULD I TELL DAD?

HOW BAD ARE WE SUPPOSING?

WELL, HYPOTHETICALLY, LET'S SAY PRETTY BAD. LIKE TO HIS CAR, HYPOTHETICALLY.

HOW BAD, HYPOTHETICALLY, TO HIS CAR?

WELL, LET'S PRETEND IT WAS *REAL* BAD.

SHOULD WE PRETEND IT COULD BE FIXED?

IF WE IMAGINED HE COULD *FIND* THE CAR, WE COULD PRETEND IT MIGHT BE FIXED.

I SEE.

YOU CAN KEEP THE BOOK. I'LL CALL THE BUS STATION.

"¿QUE PASA, SEÑORITA? ¡I AM EL FUGITIVO!"

WATTERSON

72

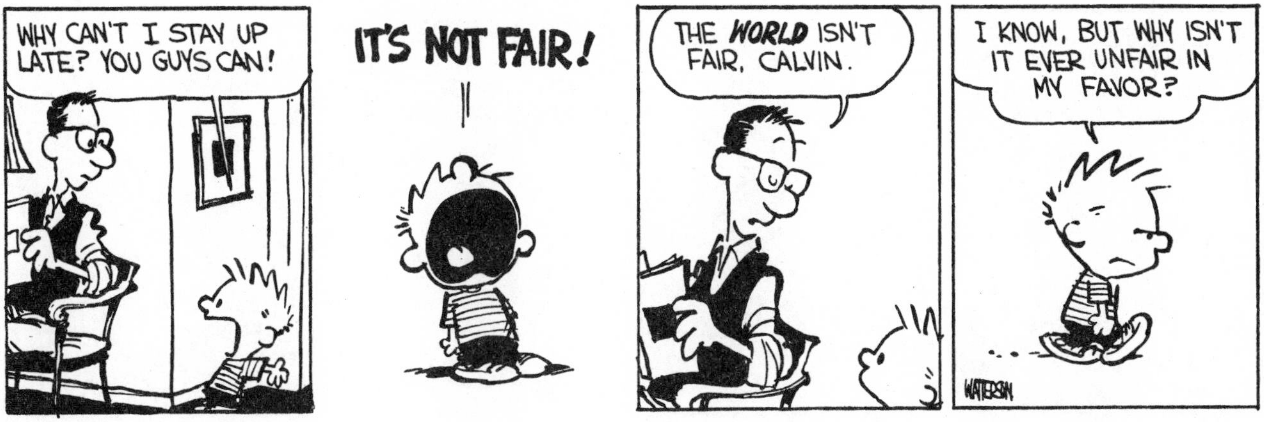
WHY CAN'T I STAY UP LATE? YOU GUYS CAN!
IT'S NOT FAIR!
THE WORLD ISN'T FAIR, CALVIN.
I KNOW, BUT WHY ISN'T IT EVER UNFAIR IN MY FAVOR?
WATTERSON

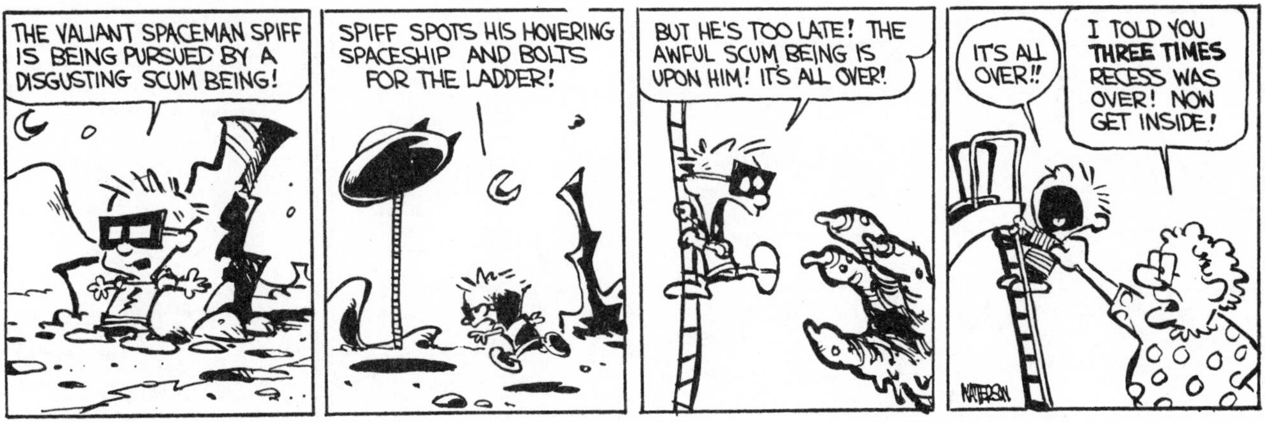
THE VALIANT SPACEMAN SPIFF IS BEING PURSUED BY A DISGUSTING SCUM BEING!
SPIFF SPOTS HIS HOVERING SPACESHIP AND BOLTS FOR THE LADDER!
BUT HE'S TOO LATE! THE AWFUL SCUM BEING IS UPON HIM! IT'S ALL OVER!
IT'S ALL OVER!!
I TOLD YOU THREE TIMES RECESS WAS OVER! NOW GET INSIDE!
WATTERSON

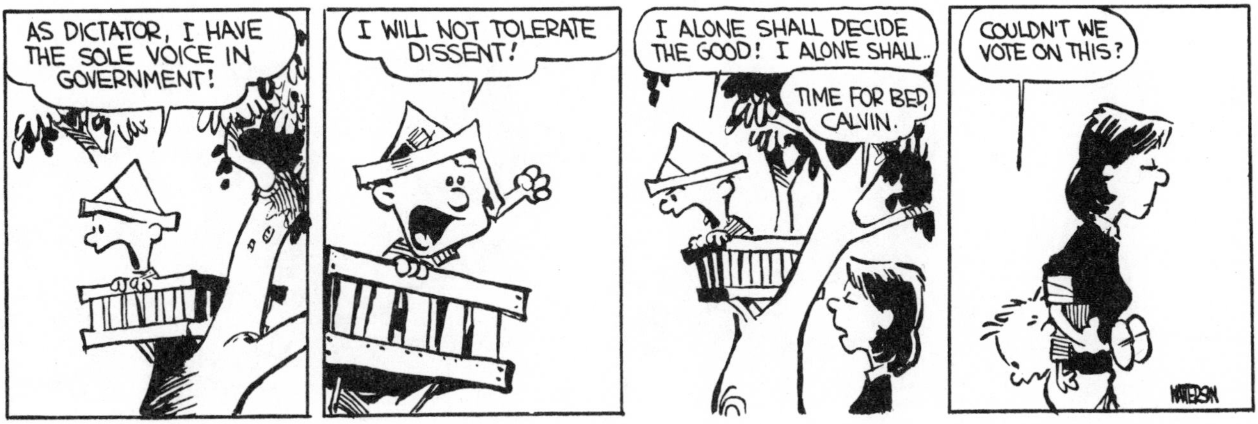
AS DICTATOR, I HAVE THE SOLE VOICE IN GOVERNMENT!
I WILL NOT TOLERATE DISSENT!
I ALONE SHALL DECIDE THE GOOD! I ALONE SHALL..
TIME FOR BED, CALVIN.
COULDN'T WE VOTE ON THIS?
WATTERSON

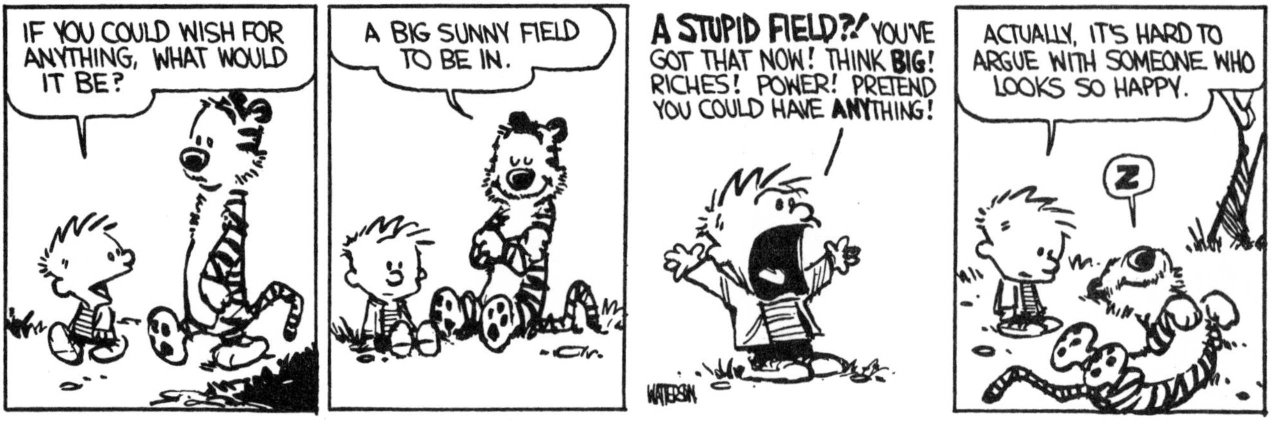
IF YOU COULD WISH FOR ANYTHING, WHAT WOULD IT BE?
A BIG SUNNY FIELD TO BE IN.
A STUPID FIELD?! YOU'VE GOT THAT NOW! THINK BIG! RICHES! POWER! PRETEND YOU COULD HAVE ANYTHING!
ACTUALLY, IT'S HARD TO ARGUE WITH SOMEONE WHO LOOKS SO HAPPY.
Z

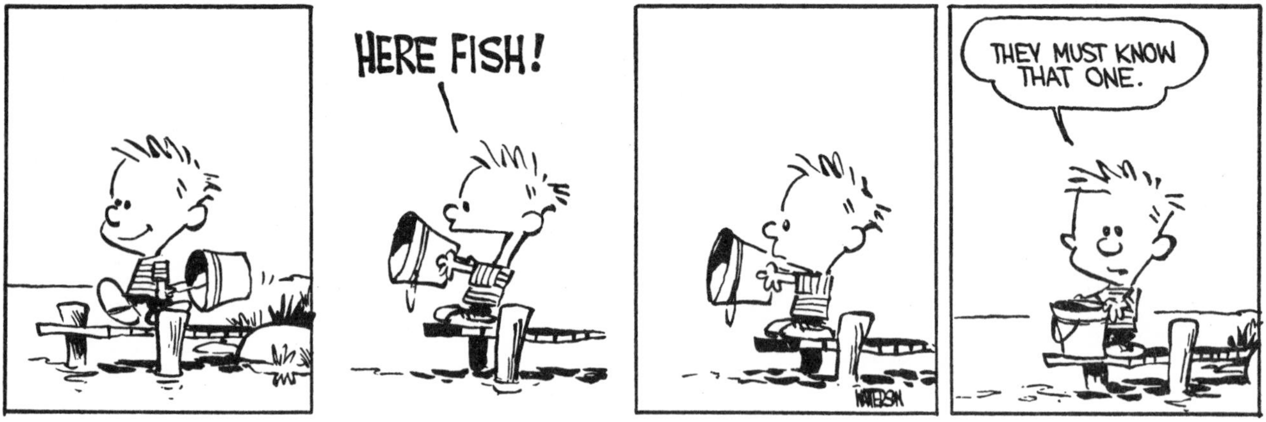
HERE FISH!
THEY MUST KNOW THAT ONE.

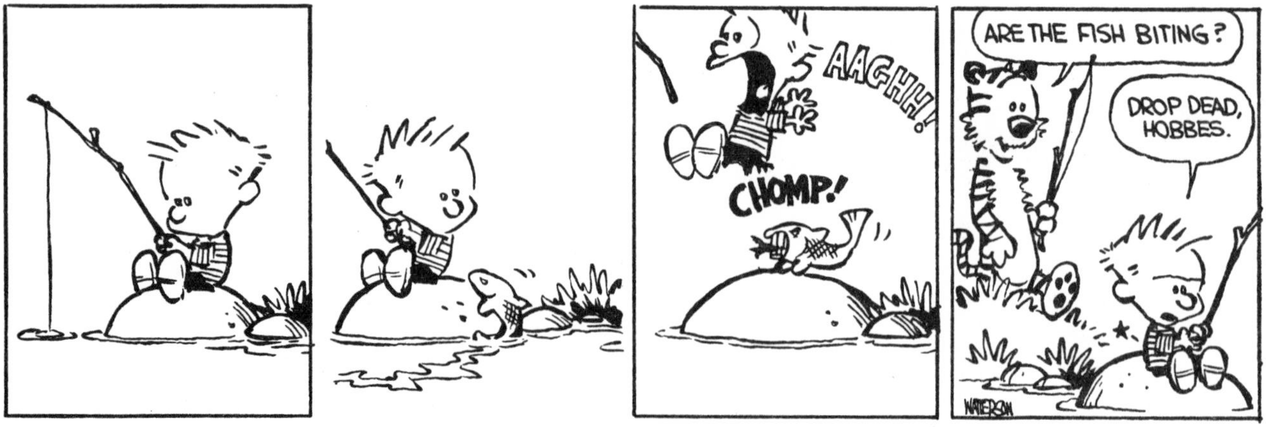
AAGHH!
CHOMP!
ARE THE FISH BITING?
DROP DEAD, HOBBES.

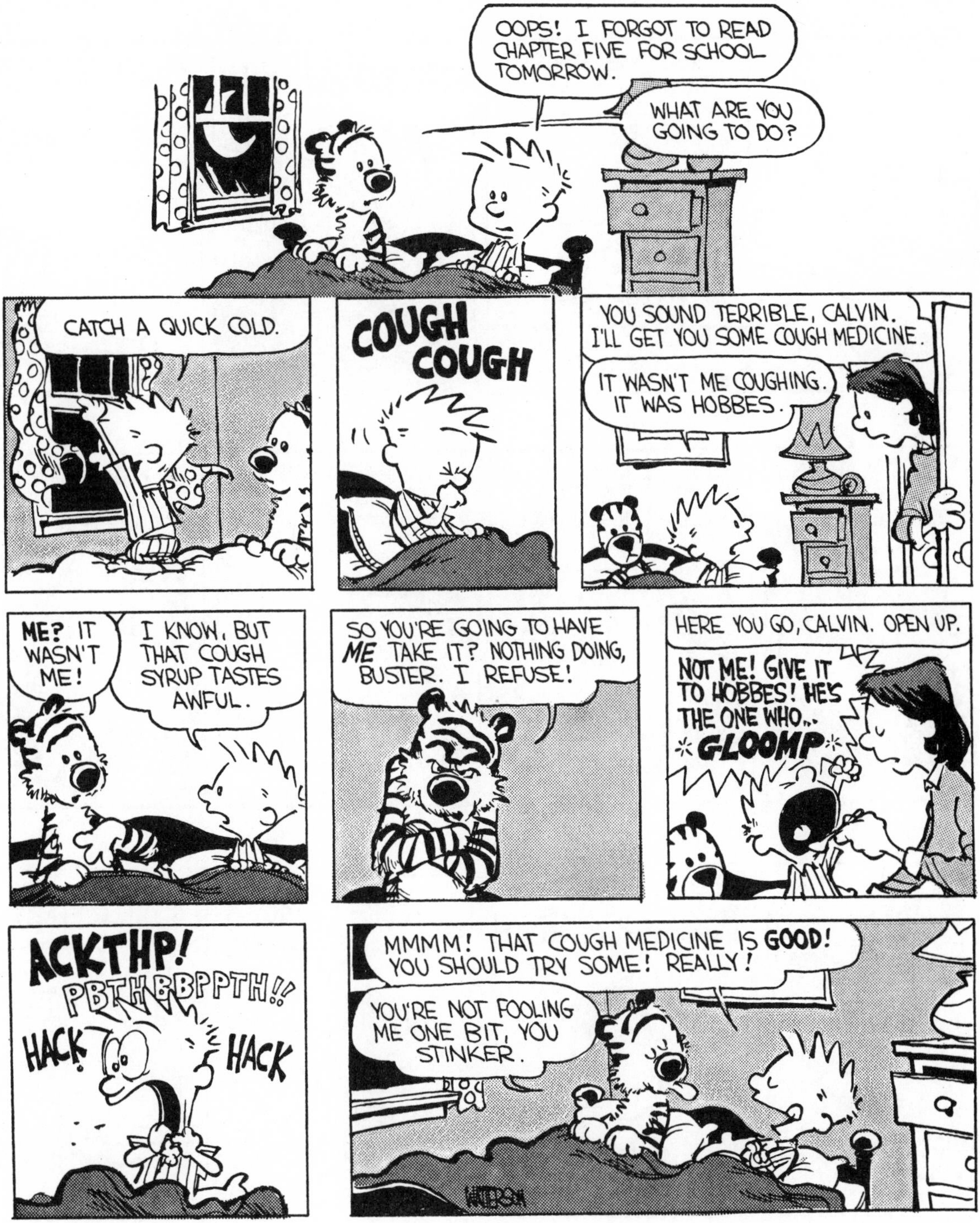

OOPS! I FORGOT TO READ CHAPTER FIVE FOR SCHOOL TOMORROW.
WHAT ARE YOU GOING TO DO?
CATCH A QUICK COLD.
COUGH COUGH
YOU SOUND TERRIBLE, CALVIN. I'LL GET YOU SOME COUGH MEDICINE.
IT WASN'T ME COUGHING. IT WAS HOBBES.
ME? IT WASN'T ME!
I KNOW, BUT THAT COUGH SYRUP TASTES AWFUL.
SO YOU'RE GOING TO HAVE ME TAKE IT? NOTHING DOING, BUSTER. I REFUSE!
HERE YOU GO, CALVIN. OPEN UP.
NOT ME! GIVE IT TO HOBBES! HE'S THE ONE WHO..
GLOOMP
ACKTHP!
PBTHBBPPTH!!
HACK
HACK
MMMM! THAT COUGH MEDICINE IS GOOD! YOU SHOULD TRY SOME! REALLY!
YOU'RE NOT FOOLING ME ONE BIT, YOU STINKER.
WATERSON

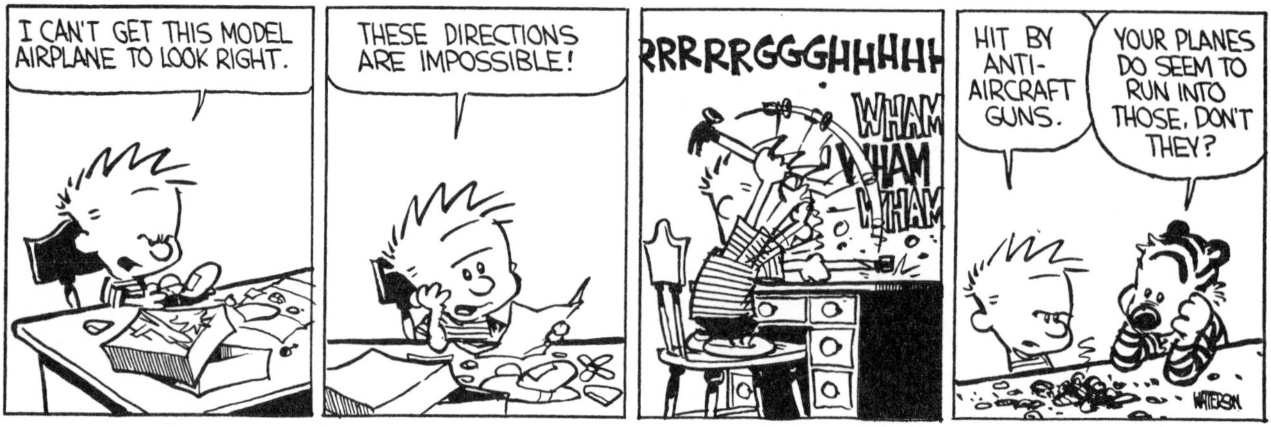
I CAN'T GET THIS MODEL AIRPLANE TO LOOK RIGHT.
THESE DIRECTIONS ARE IMPOSSIBLE!
RRRRRGGGHHHHH
WHAM WHAM WHAM
HIT BY ANTI-AIRCRAFT GUNS.
YOUR PLANES DO SEEM TO RUN INTO THOSE, DON'T THEY?
WATTERSON

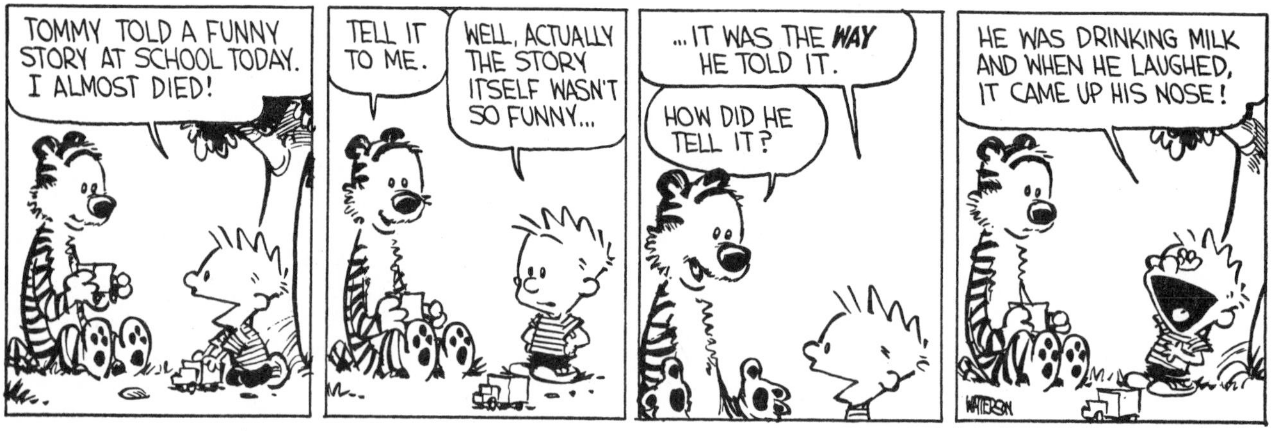
TOMMY TOLD A FUNNY STORY AT SCHOOL TODAY. I ALMOST DIED!
TELL IT TO ME.
WELL, ACTUALLY THE STORY ITSELF WASN'T SO FUNNY...
...IT WAS THE WAY HE TOLD IT.
HOW DID HE TELL IT?
HE WAS DRINKING MILK AND WHEN HE LAUGHED, IT CAME UP HIS NOSE!
WATTERSON

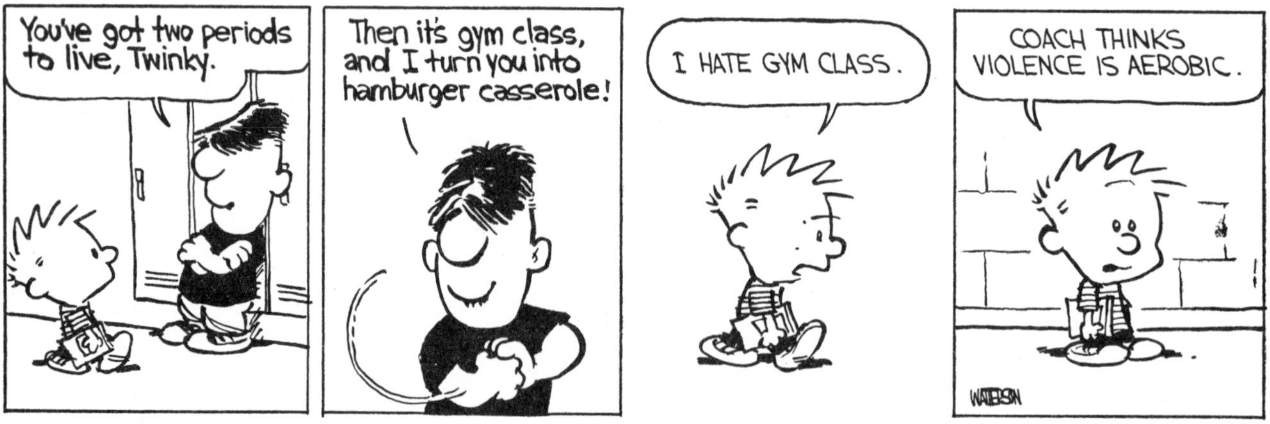
You've got two periods to live, Twinky.
Then it's gym class, and I turn you into hamburger casserole!
I HATE GYM CLASS.
COACH THINKS VIOLENCE IS AEROBIC.
WATTERSON

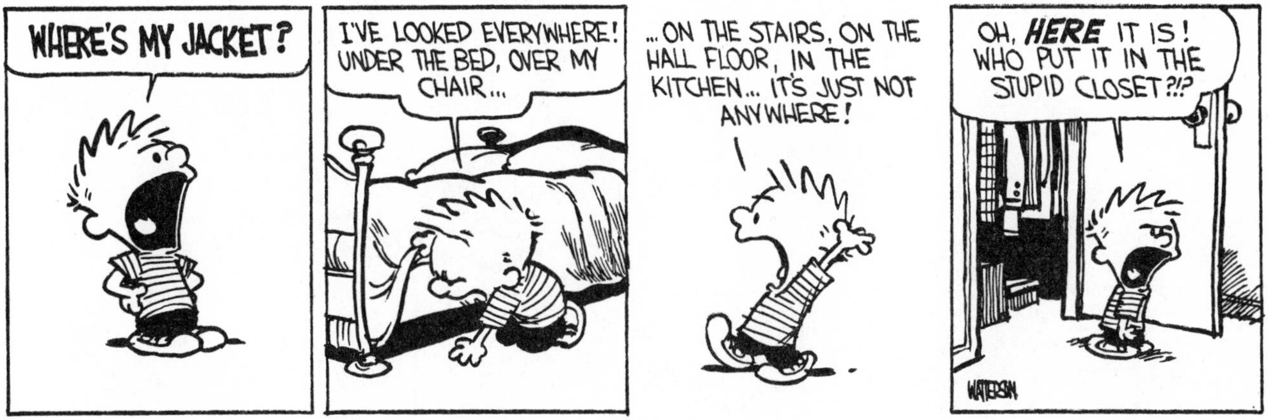
WHERE'S MY JACKET?
I'VE LOOKED EVERYWHERE! UNDER THE BED, OVER MY CHAIR...
...ON THE STAIRS, ON THE HALL FLOOR, IN THE KITCHEN... IT'S JUST NOT ANYWHERE!
OH, HERE IT IS! WHO PUT IT IN THE STUPID CLOSET?!?
WATERSON

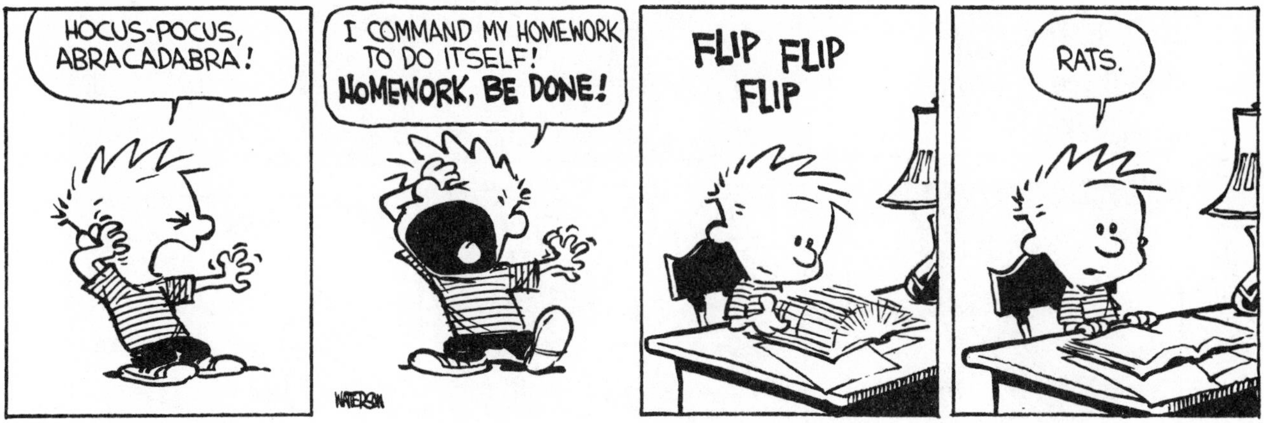
HOCUS-POCUS, ABRACADABRA!
I COMMAND MY HOMEWORK TO DO ITSELF! HOMEWORK, BE DONE!
WATERSON
FLIP FLIP FLIP
RATS.

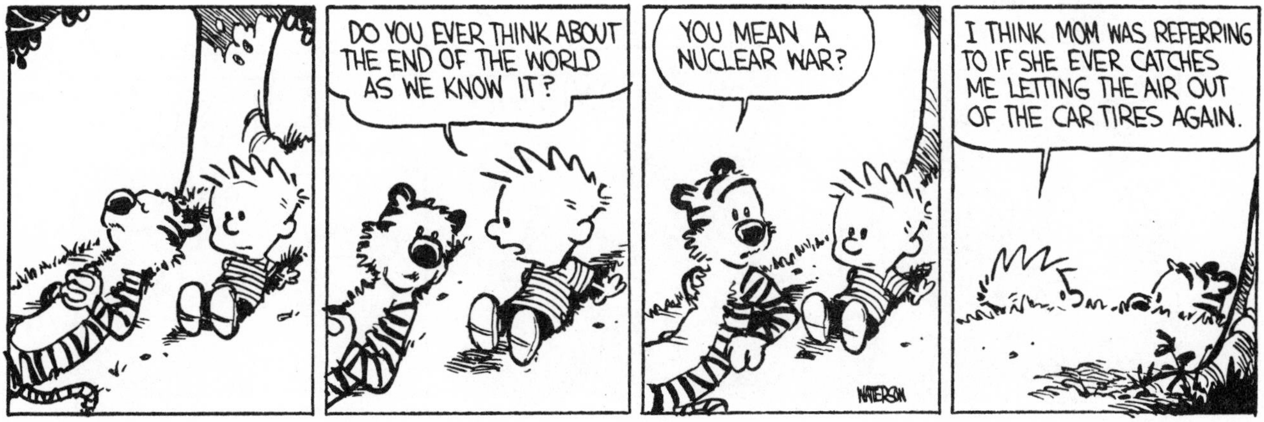
DO YOU EVER THINK ABOUT THE END OF THE WORLD AS WE KNOW IT?
YOU MEAN A NUCLEAR WAR?
WATERSON
I THINK MOM WAS REFERRING TO IF SHE EVER CATCHES ME LETTING THE AIR OUT OF THE CAR TIRES AGAIN.

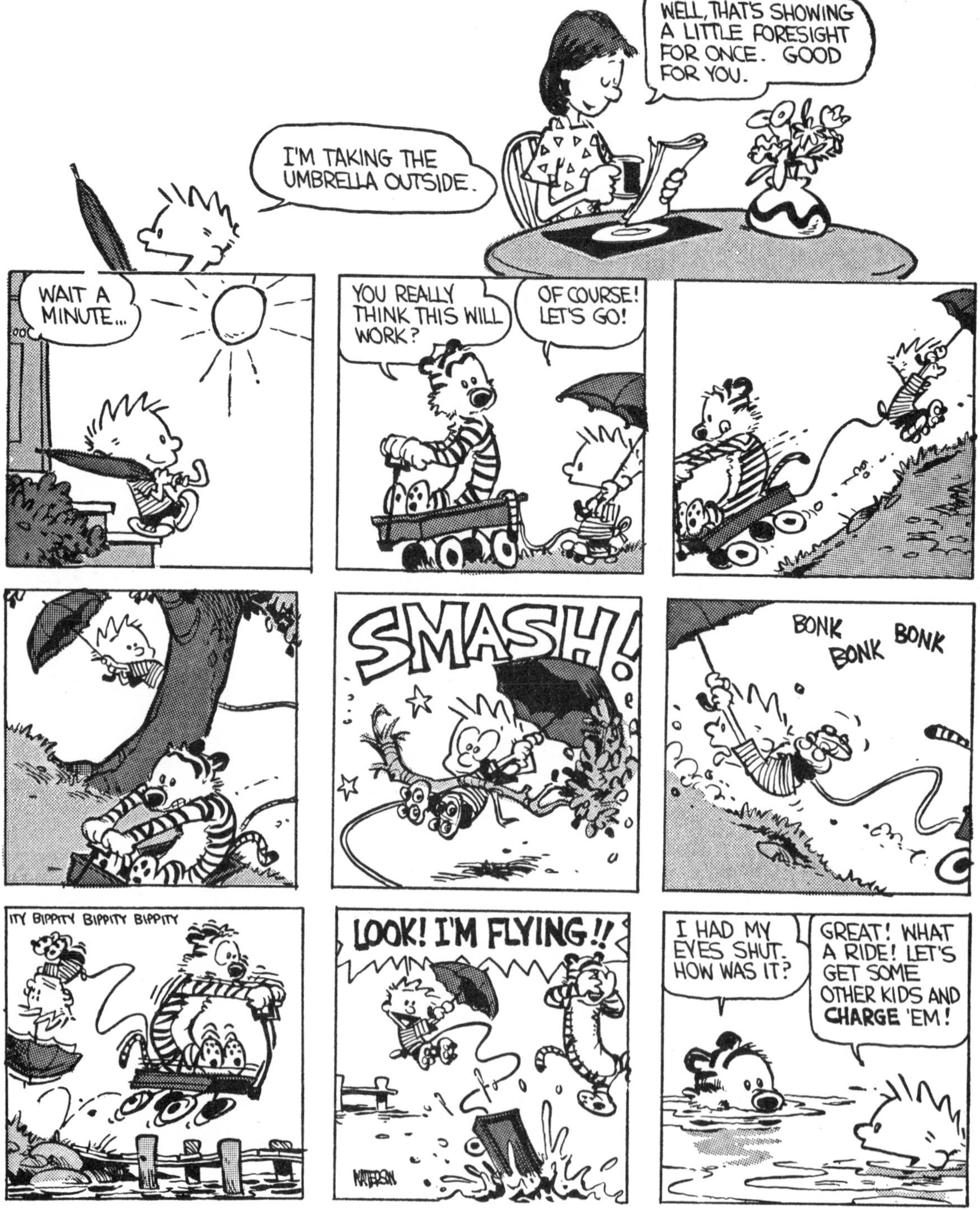
I'M TAKING THE UMBRELLA OUTSIDE.
WELL, THAT'S SHOWING A LITTLE FORESIGHT FOR ONCE. GOOD FOR YOU.
WAIT A MINUTE...
YOU REALLY THINK THIS WILL WORK?
OF COURSE! LET'S GO!
SMASH!
BONK
BONK
BONK
ITY BIPPITY BIPPITY BIPPITY
LOOK! I'M FLYING!!
I HAD MY EYES SHUT. HOW WAS IT?
GREAT! WHAT A RIDE! LET'S GET SOME OTHER KIDS AND **CHARGE** 'EM!

79

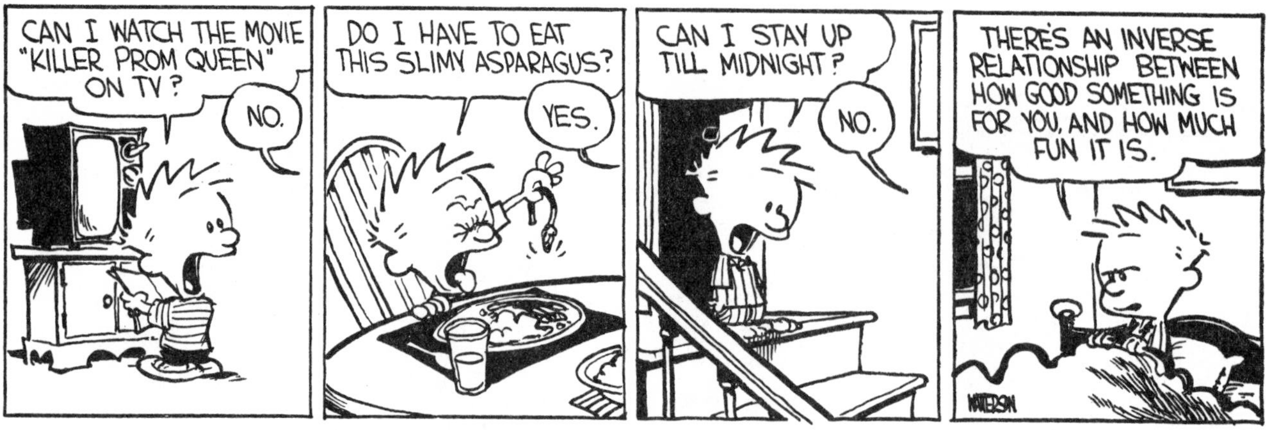
CAN I WATCH THE MOVIE "KILLER PROM QUEEN" ON TV?
NO.
DO I HAVE TO EAT THIS SLIMY ASPARAGUS?
YES.
CAN I STAY UP TILL MIDNIGHT?
NO.
THERE'S AN INVERSE RELATIONSHIP BETWEEN HOW GOOD SOMETHING IS FOR YOU, AND HOW MUCH FUN IT IS.

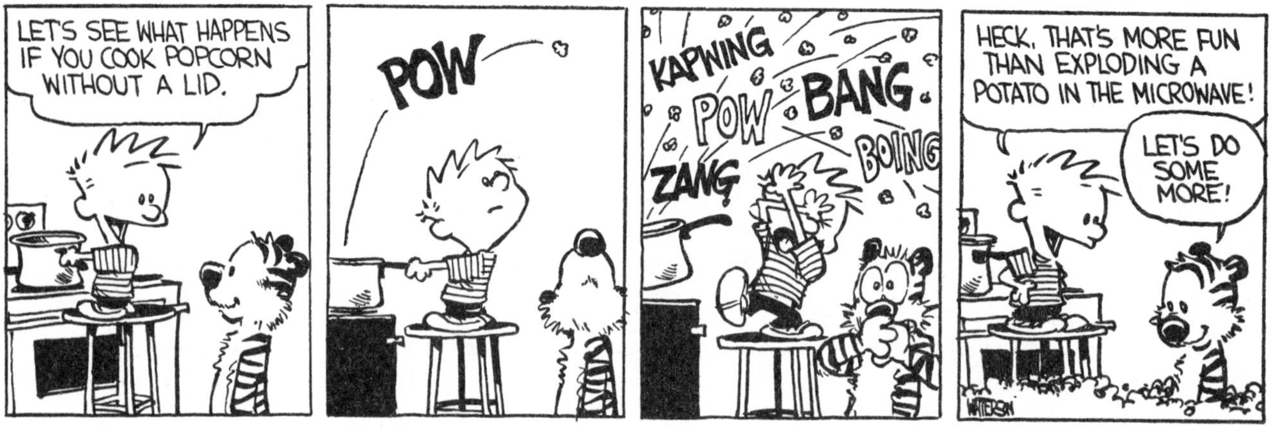
LET'S SEE WHAT HAPPENS IF YOU COOK POPCORN WITHOUT A LID.
POW
KAPWING
POW
BANG
ZANG
BOING
HECK, THAT'S MORE FUN THAN EXPLODING A POTATO IN THE MICROWAVE!
LET'S DO SOME MORE!

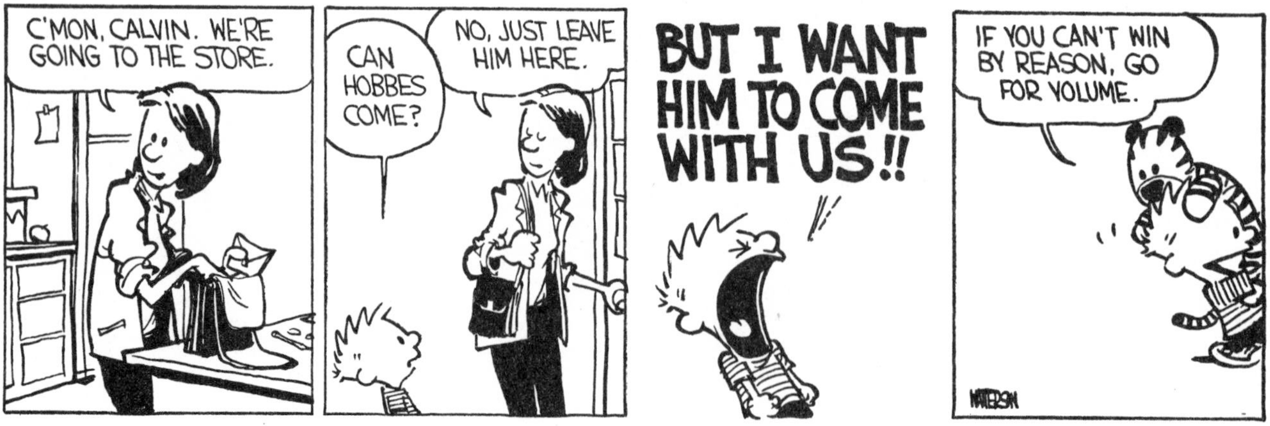
C'MON, CALVIN. WE'RE GOING TO THE STORE.
CAN HOBBES COME?
NO, JUST LEAVE HIM HERE.
BUT I WANT HIM TO COME WITH US!!
IF YOU CAN'T WIN BY REASON, GO FOR VOLUME.

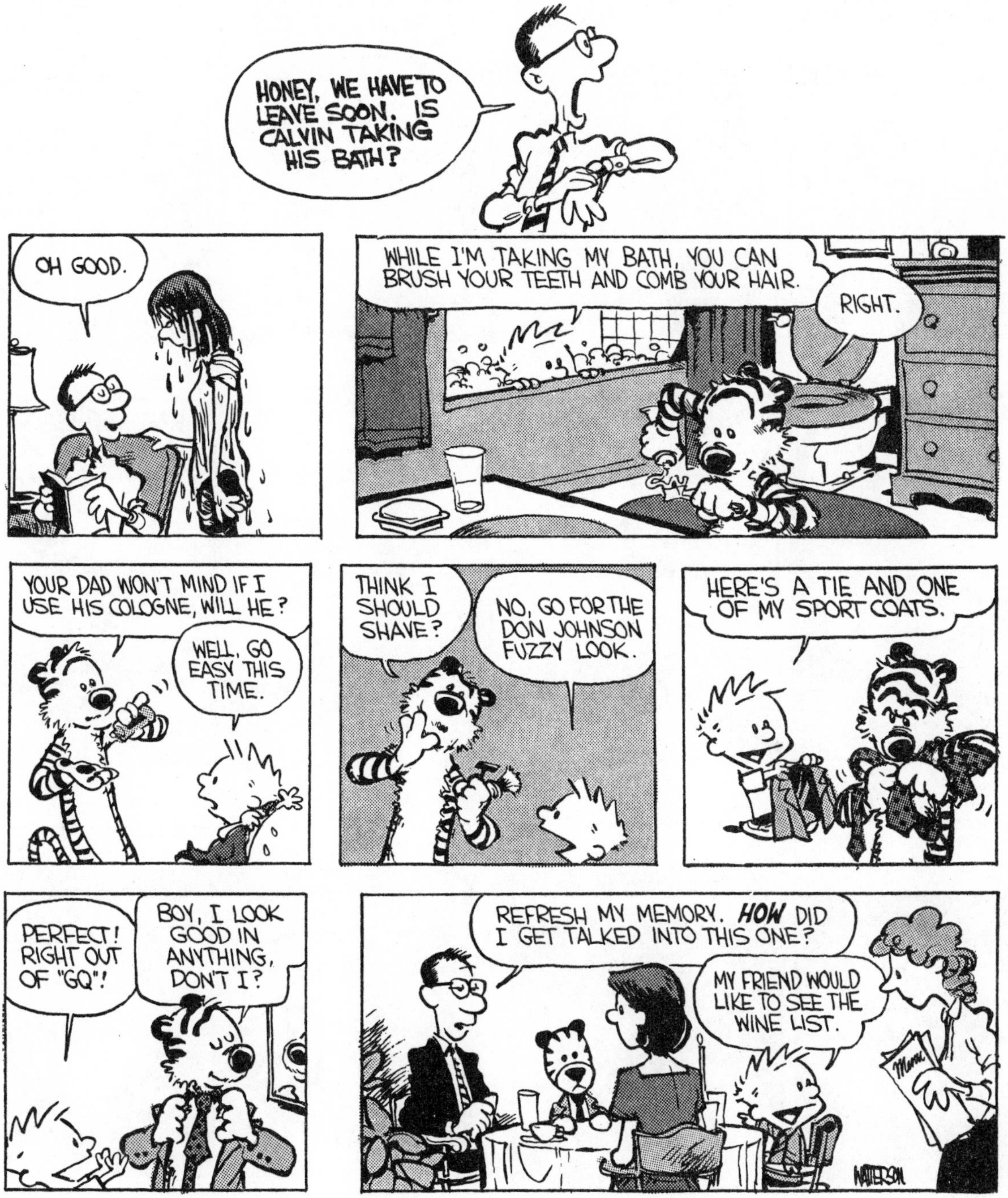
HONEY, WE HAVE TO LEAVE SOON. IS CALVIN TAKING HIS BATH?
OH GOOD.
WHILE I'M TAKING MY BATH, YOU CAN BRUSH YOUR TEETH AND COMB YOUR HAIR.
RIGHT.
YOUR DAD WON'T MIND IF I USE HIS COLOGNE, WILL HE?
WELL, GO EASY THIS TIME.
THINK I SHOULD SHAVE?
NO, GO FOR THE DON JOHNSON FUZZY LOOK.
HERE'S A TIE AND ONE OF MY SPORT COATS.
PERFECT! RIGHT OUT OF "GQ"!
BOY, I LOOK GOOD IN ANYTHING, DON'T I?
REFRESH MY MEMORY. HOW DID I GET TALKED INTO THIS ONE?
MY FRIEND WOULD LIKE TO SEE THE WINE LIST.
Menu
WATTERSON

SO THE CONTRACTOR SAYS IT WILL COST ABOUT $200 TO FIX.

OH, THAT DUMB KID!

WELL, IT'S ALL PART OF RAISING A CHILD, RIGHT?

MM.

YOU'RE NOT SORRY WE HAD CALVIN, ARE YOU?

ARE *YOU*?

I ASKED FIRST....BESIDES, IT WASN'T ALL *MY* DECISION.

ALL *I* KNOW IS THAT *I* OFFERED TO BUY US A DACHSHUND, BUT NO, *YOU* SAID...

DO YOU THINK THERE'S A GOD?

WELL *SOME*BODY'S OUT TO GET ME.

SPACEMAN SPIFF CLOSES IN ON THE ALIEN VESSEL!

THE ALIEN, BEING UNNATURALLY STUPID, IS BLISSFULLY IGNORANT OF ITS IMMINENT DOOM!

OUR HERO LOCKS ONTO TARGET AND WARMS UP HIS FRAP-RAY BLASTER!

MISS WORMWOOD!!

ZOUNDS! A GORKON DEATH STATION APPEARS! EVASIVE ACTION!

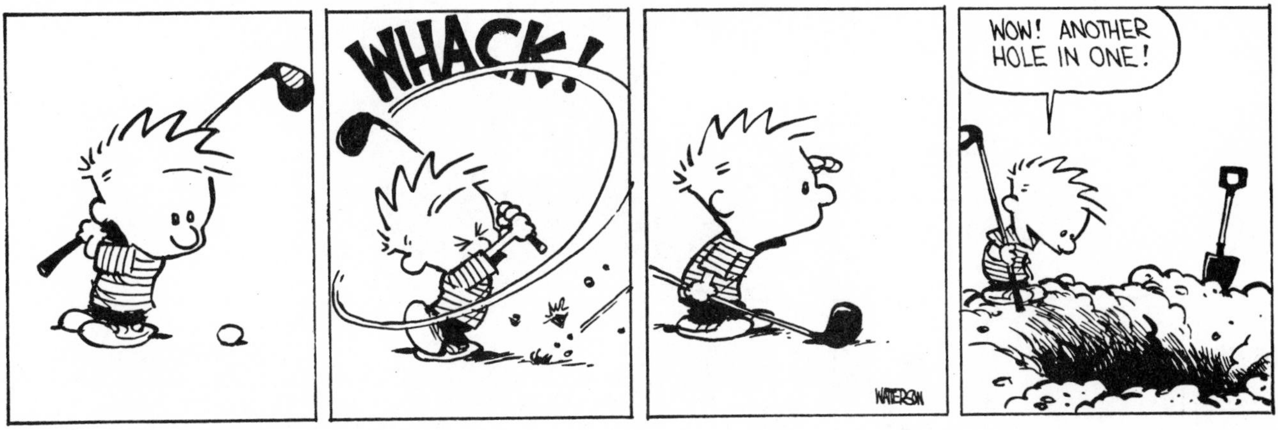
WHACK!
WOW! ANOTHER HOLE IN ONE!

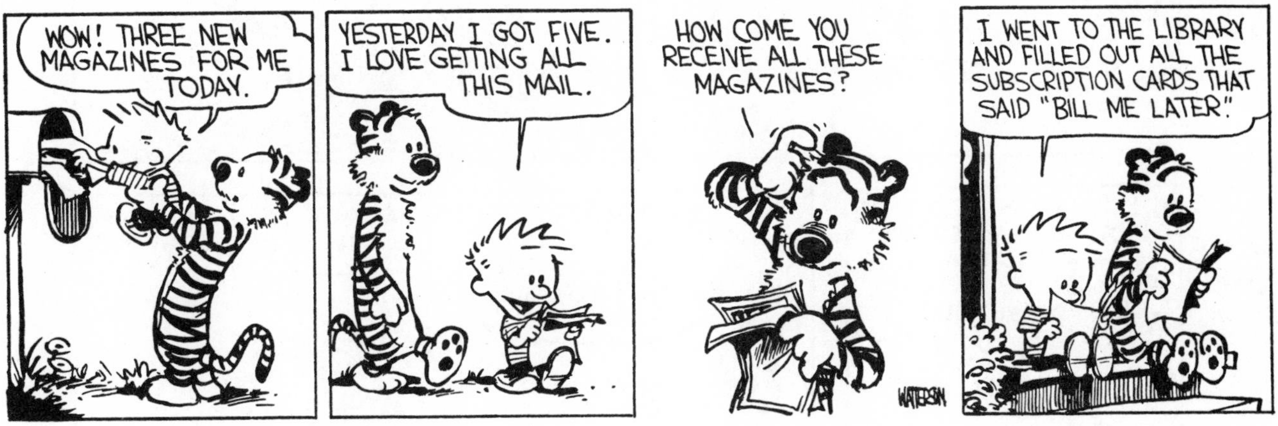
WOW! THREE NEW MAGAZINES FOR ME TODAY.
YESTERDAY I GOT FIVE. I LOVE GETTING ALL THIS MAIL.
HOW COME YOU RECEIVE ALL THESE MAGAZINES?
I WENT TO THE LIBRARY AND FILLED OUT ALL THE SUBSCRIPTION CARDS THAT SAID "BILL ME LATER."

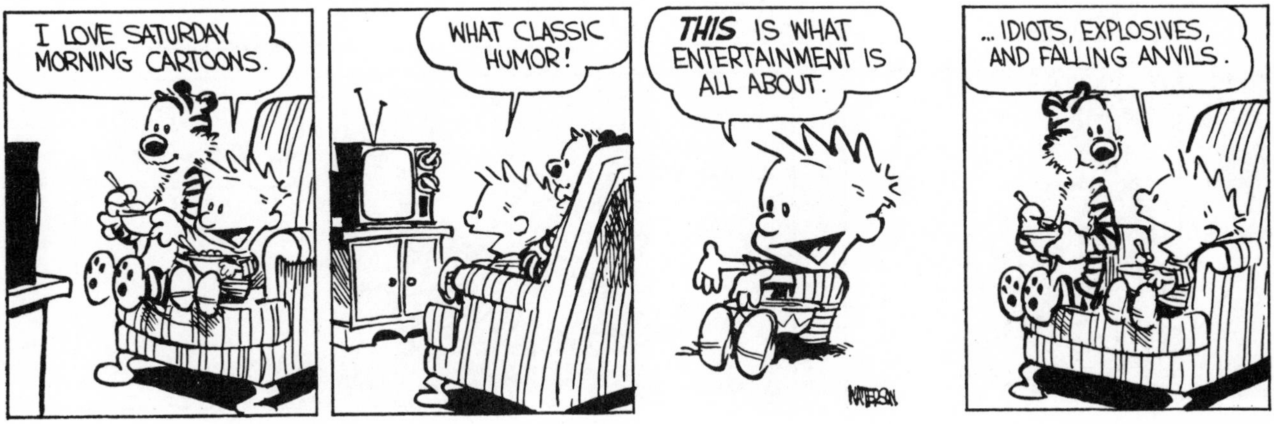
I LOVE SATURDAY MORNING CARTOONS.
WHAT CLASSIC HUMOR!
THIS IS WHAT ENTERTAINMENT IS ALL ABOUT.
...IDIOTS, EXPLOSIVES, AND FALLING ANVILS.

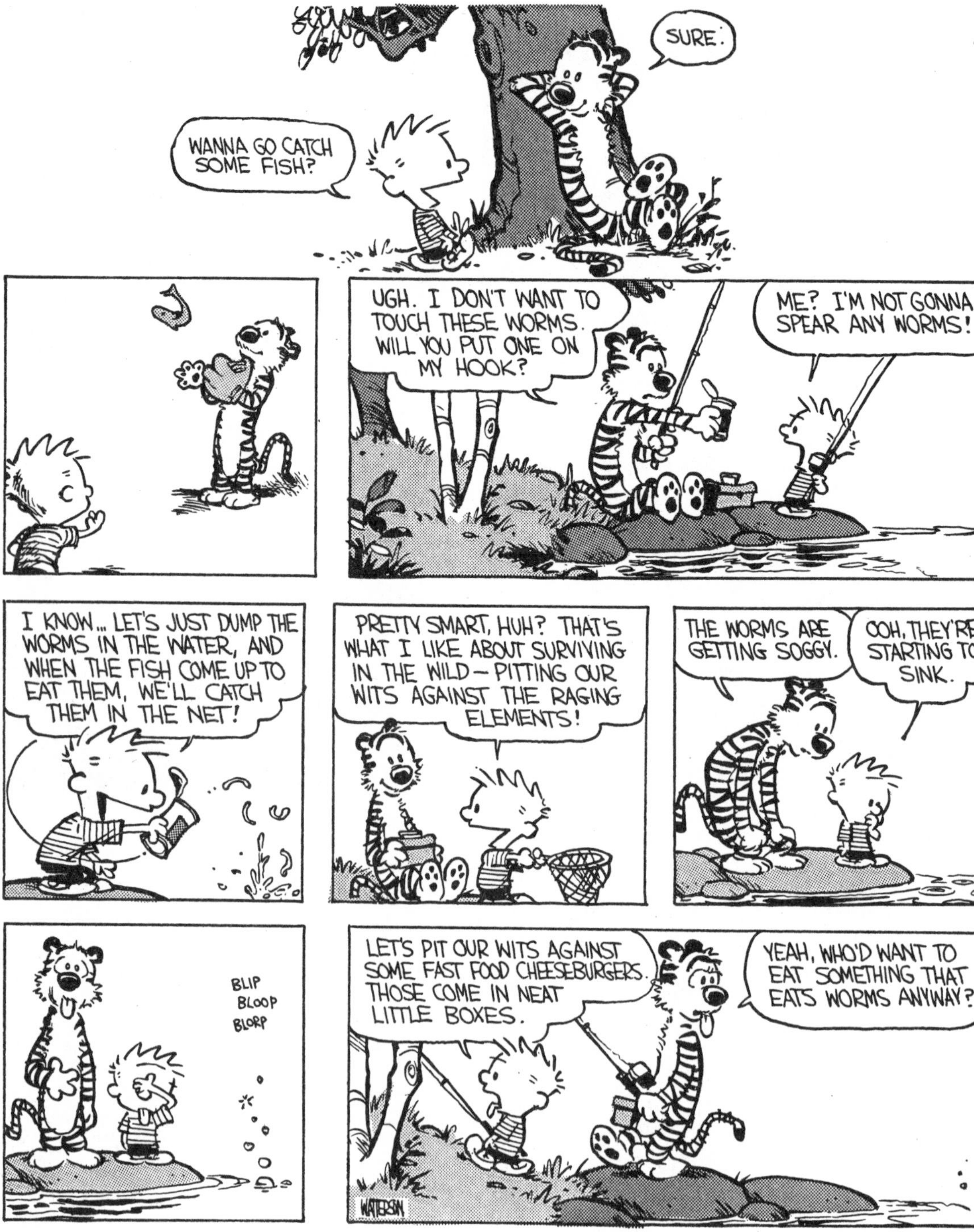
WANNA GO CATCH SOME FISH?
SURE.
UGH. I DON'T WANT TO TOUCH THESE WORMS. WILL YOU PUT ONE ON MY HOOK?
ME? I'M NOT GONNA SPEAR ANY WORMS!
I KNOW... LET'S JUST DUMP THE WORMS IN THE WATER, AND WHEN THE FISH COME UP TO EAT THEM, WE'LL CATCH THEM IN THE NET!
PRETTY SMART, HUH? THAT'S WHAT I LIKE ABOUT SURVIVING IN THE WILD—PITTING OUR WITS AGAINST THE RAGING ELEMENTS!
THE WORMS ARE GETTING SOGGY.
OOH, THEY'RE STARTING TO SINK.
BLIP
BLOOP
BLORP
LET'S PIT OUR WITS AGAINST SOME FAST FOOD CHEESEBURGERS. THOSE COME IN NEAT LITTLE BOXES.
YEAH, WHO'D WANT TO EAT SOMETHING THAT EATS WORMS ANYWAY?
WATTERSON

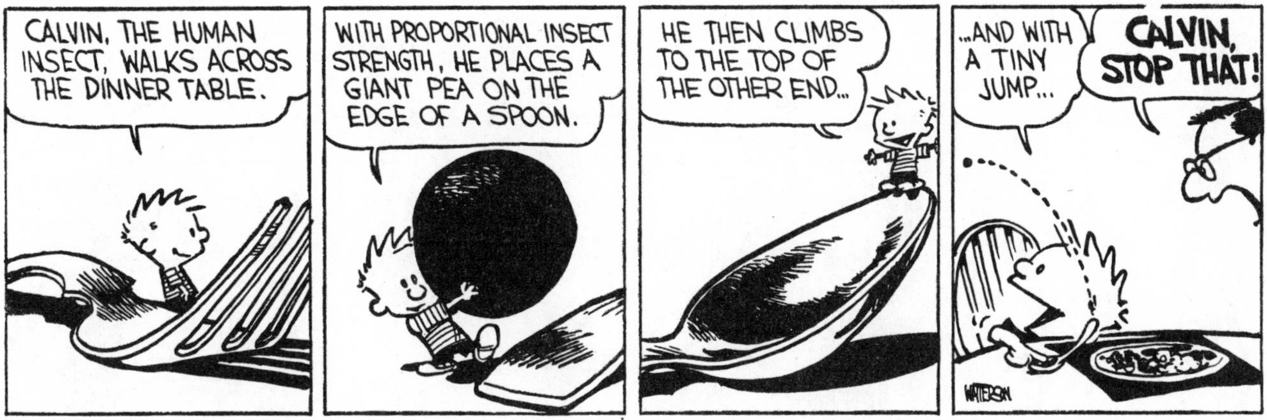
CALVIN, THE HUMAN INSECT, WALKS ACROSS THE DINNER TABLE.
WITH PROPORTIONAL INSECT STRENGTH, HE PLACES A GIANT PEA ON THE EDGE OF A SPOON.
HE THEN CLIMBS TO THE TOP OF THE OTHER END...
...AND WITH A TINY JUMP...
CALVIN, STOP THAT!

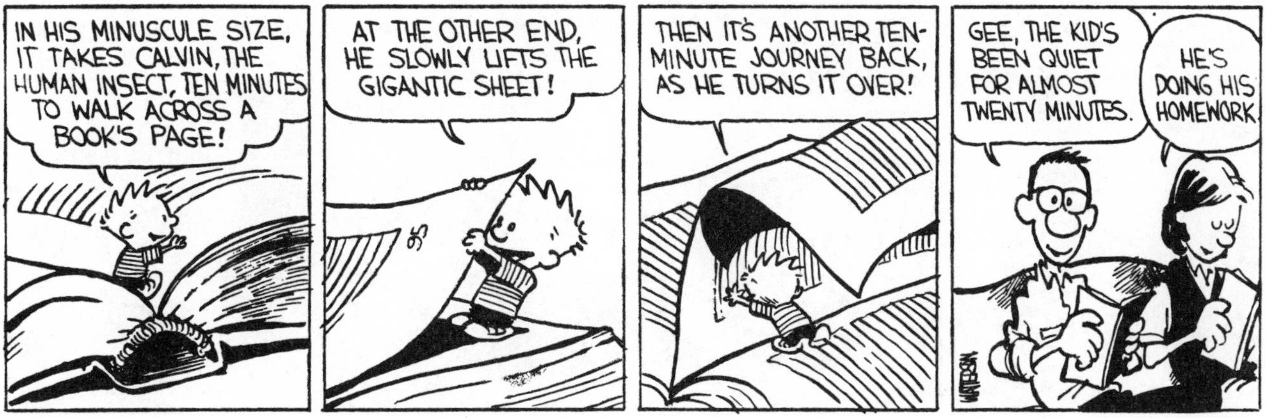
IN HIS MINUSCULE SIZE, IT TAKES CALVIN, THE HUMAN INSECT, TEN MINUTES TO WALK ACROSS A BOOK'S PAGE!
AT THE OTHER END, HE SLOWLY LIFTS THE GIGANTIC SHEET!
95
THEN IT'S ANOTHER TEN-MINUTE JOURNEY BACK, AS HE TURNS IT OVER!
GEE, THE KID'S BEEN QUIET FOR ALMOST TWENTY MINUTES.
HE'S DOING HIS HOMEWORK.

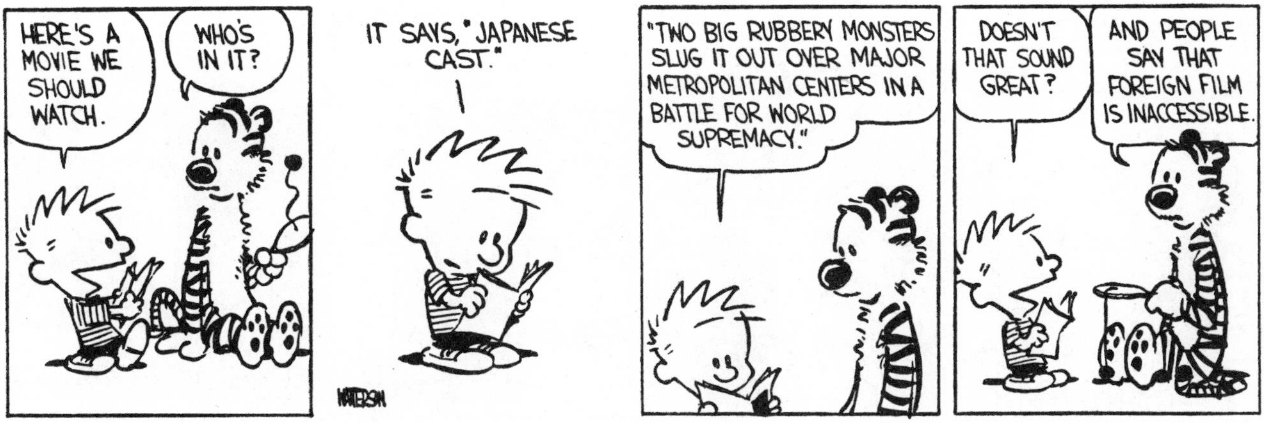
HERE'S A MOVIE WE SHOULD WATCH.
WHO'S IN IT?
IT SAYS, "JAPANESE CAST."
"TWO BIG RUBBERY MONSTERS SLUG IT OUT OVER MAJOR METROPOLITAN CENTERS IN A BATTLE FOR WORLD SUPREMACY."
DOESN'T THAT SOUND GREAT?
AND PEOPLE SAY THAT FOREIGN FILM IS INACCESSIBLE.

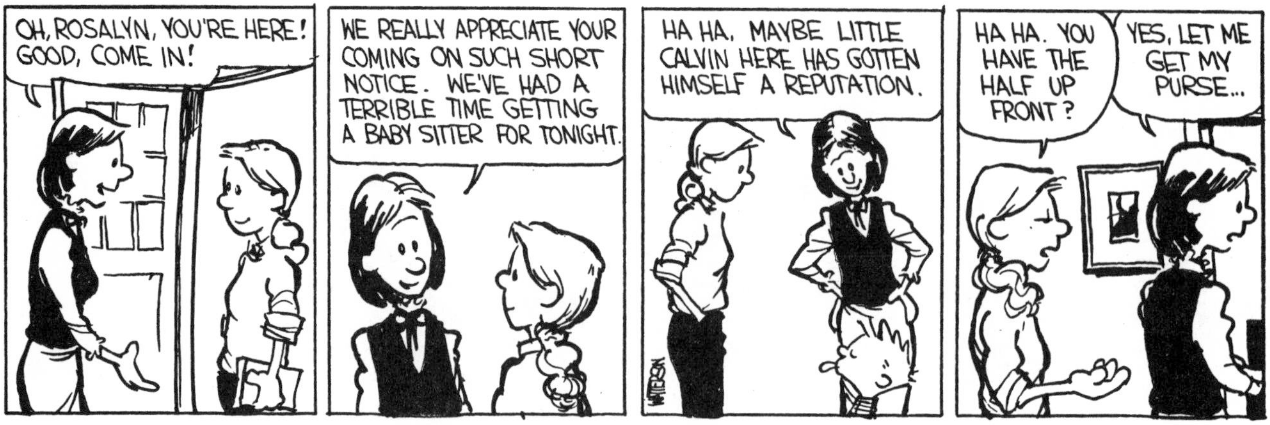
OH, ROSALYN, YOU'RE HERE! GOOD, COME IN!
WE REALLY APPRECIATE YOUR COMING ON SUCH SHORT NOTICE. WE'VE HAD A TERRIBLE TIME GETTING A BABY SITTER FOR TONIGHT.
HA HA. MAYBE LITTLE CALVIN HERE HAS GOTTEN HIMSELF A REPUTATION.
HA HA. YOU HAVE THE HALF UP FRONT?
YES, LET ME GET MY PURSE...
WATTERSON

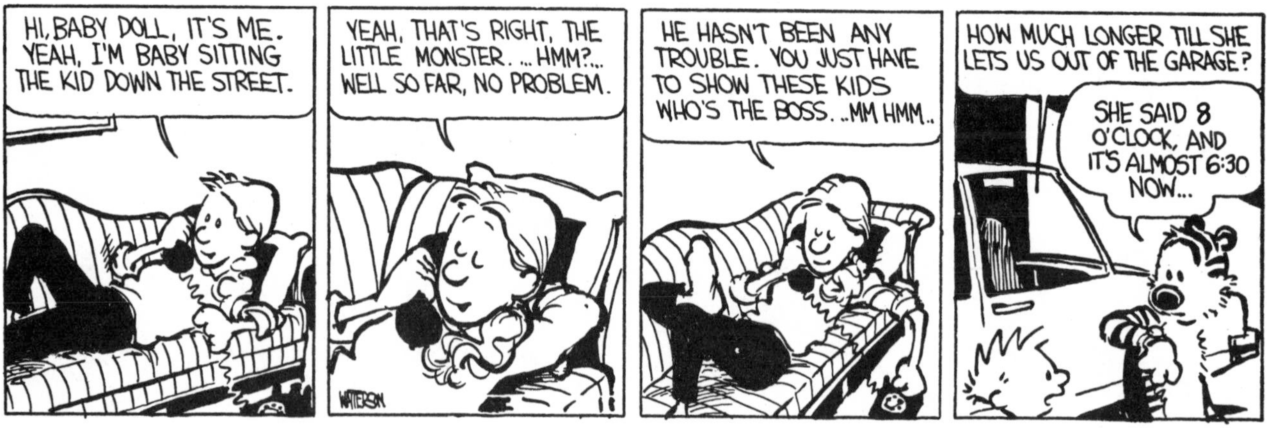
HI, BABY DOLL, IT'S ME. YEAH, I'M BABY SITTING THE KID DOWN THE STREET.
YEAH, THAT'S RIGHT, THE LITTLE MONSTER. ...HMM?... WELL SO FAR, NO PROBLEM.
HE HASN'T BEEN ANY TROUBLE. YOU JUST HAVE TO SHOW THESE KIDS WHO'S THE BOSS. ..MM HMM..
HOW MUCH LONGER TILL SHE LETS US OUT OF THE GARAGE?
SHE SAID 8 O'CLOCK, AND IT'S ALMOST 6:30 NOW...
WATTERSON

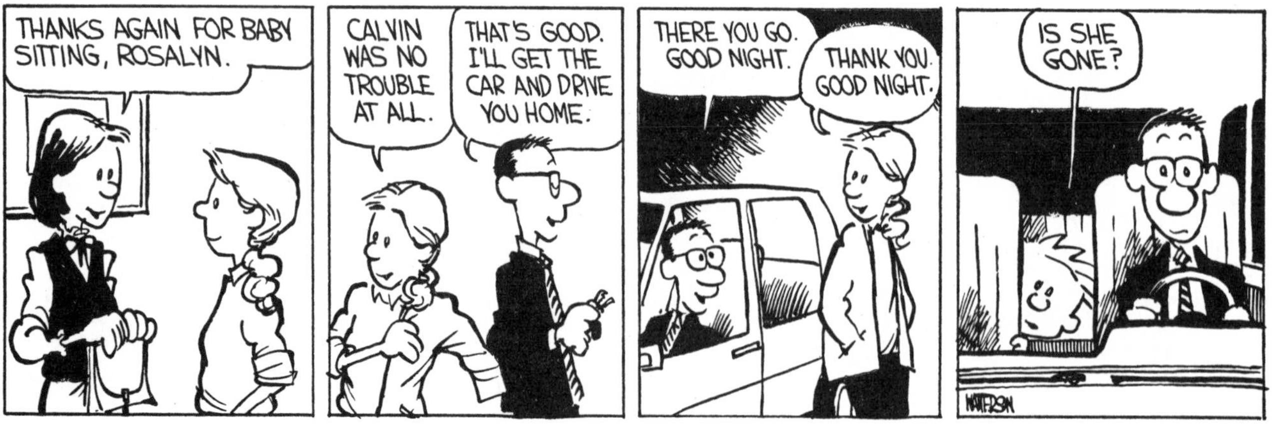
THANKS AGAIN FOR BABY SITTING, ROSALYN.
CALVIN WAS NO TROUBLE AT ALL.
THAT'S GOOD. I'LL GET THE CAR AND DRIVE YOU HOME.
THERE YOU GO. GOOD NIGHT.
THANK YOU. GOOD NIGHT.
IS SHE GONE?
WATTERSON

88

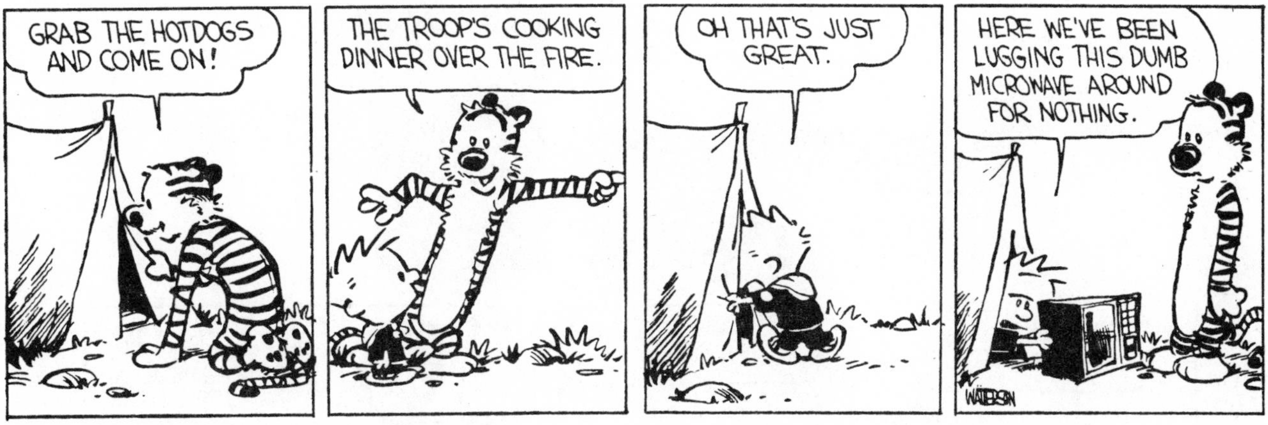
GRAB THE HOTDOGS AND COME ON!
THE TROOP'S COOKING DINNER OVER THE FIRE.
OH THAT'S JUST GREAT.
HERE WE'VE BEEN LUGGING THIS DUMB MICROWAVE AROUND FOR NOTHING.

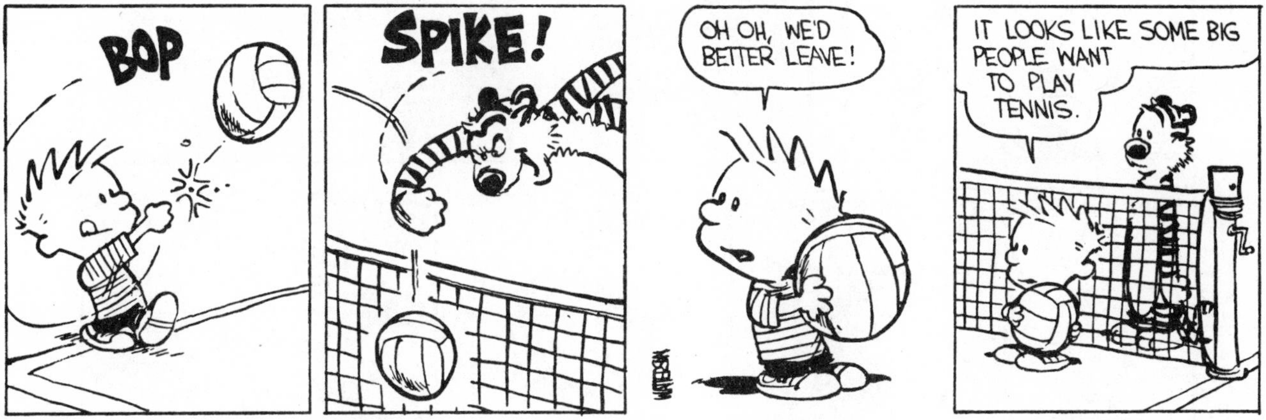
BOP
SPIKE!
OH OH, WE'D BETTER LEAVE!
IT LOOKS LIKE SOME BIG PEOPLE WANT TO PLAY TENNIS.

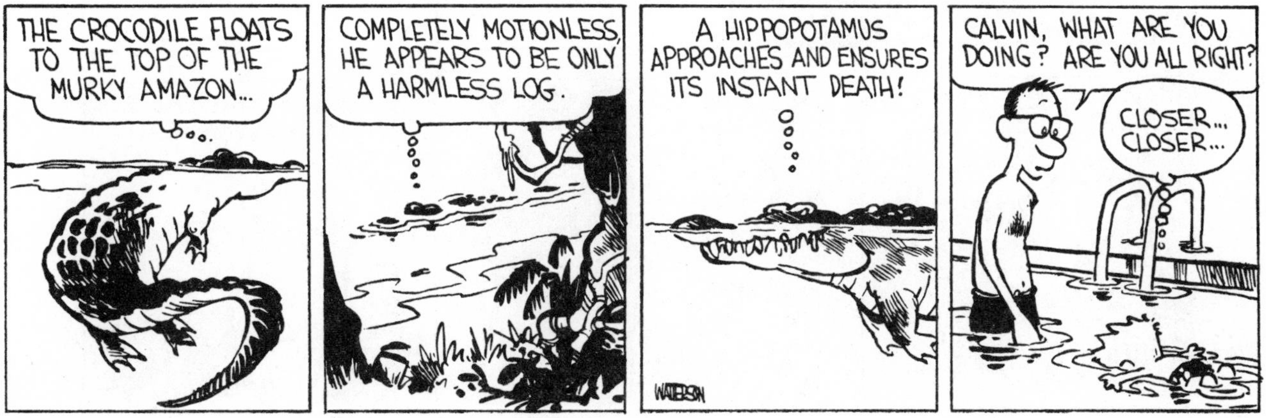
THE CROCODILE FLOATS TO THE TOP OF THE MURKY AMAZON...
COMPLETELY MOTIONLESS, HE APPEARS TO BE ONLY A HARMLESS LOG.
A HIPPOPOTAMUS APPROACHES AND ENSURES ITS INSTANT DEATH!
CALVIN, WHAT ARE YOU DOING? ARE YOU ALL RIGHT?
CLOSER... CLOSER...

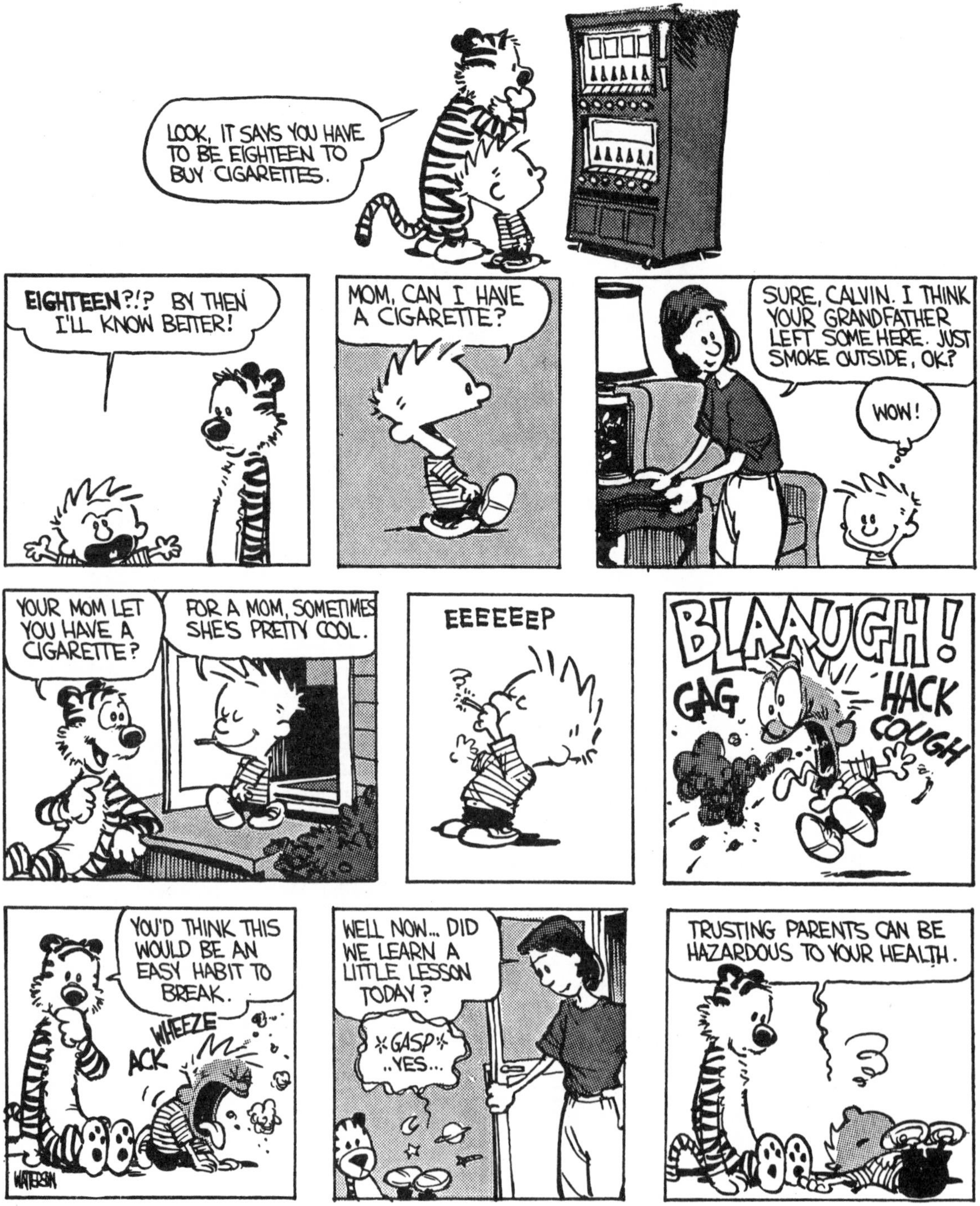
LOOK, IT SAYS YOU HAVE TO BE EIGHTEEN TO BUY CIGARETTES.
EIGHTEEN?!? BY THEN I'LL KNOW BETTER!
MOM, CAN I HAVE A CIGARETTE?
SURE, CALVIN. I THINK YOUR GRANDFATHER LEFT SOME HERE. JUST SMOKE OUTSIDE, OK?
WOW!
YOUR MOM LET YOU HAVE A CIGARETTE?
FOR A MOM, SOMETIMES SHE'S PRETTY COOL.
EEEEEEP
BLAAUGH!
GAG
HACK
COUGH
YOU'D THINK THIS WOULD BE AN EASY HABIT TO BREAK.
WHEEZE
ACK
WATERSON
WELL NOW... DID WE LEARN A LITTLE LESSON TODAY?
GASP ..YES...
TRUSTING PARENTS CAN BE HAZARDOUS TO YOUR HEALTH.

MOM! MOM! A BIG DOG KNOCKED ME DOWN AND HE STOLE HOBBES!

I TRIED TO CATCH HIM, BUT I COULDN'T, AND NOW I'VE LOST MY BEST FRIEND!

WELL CALVIN, IF YOU WOULDN'T DRAG THAT TIGER EVERYWHERE, THINGS LIKE THIS WOULDN'T HAPPEN.

THERE'S NO PROBLEM SO AWFUL THAT YOU CAN'T ADD SOME GUILT TO IT AND MAKE IT EVEN WORSE!

I CAN'T SLEEP AT ALL. POOR HOBBES! I WONDER WHERE HE IS. I HOPE HE'S OK.

SNIFF.. WHAT DID I EVER DO TO DESERVE THIS?

WHATEVER IT WAS, I'M *SORRY* ALREADY!

LOST: MY TIGER, "HOBBES"

MAYBE YOU SHOULD DESCRIBE HIM.

ON THE QUIET SIDE. SOMEWHAT PECULIAR. A GOOD COMPANION, IN A WEIRD SORT OF WAY.

I MEAN, WHAT DOES HE LOOK LIKE?

OH.

WELL LOOK, SOMEBODY LEFT A STUFFED TIGER OUT IN THE FIELD. HOW STRANGE.

LOOKS LIKE A DOG'S BEEN CHEWING ON YOU, FELLA.

WELL, NOTHING A LITTLE TEA PARTY WITH SOME OTHER STUFFED ANIMALS WOULDN'T HELP. C'MON.

HOBBES! HOBBES! WHERE ARE YOU ??

HELLO, CALVIN. WOULD YOU LIKE TO JOIN MY TEA PARTY?

HECK NO. I'M TRYING TO FIND MY BEST FRIEND, WHO'S BEEN KIDNAPPED BY A DOG. LEAVE ME ALONE.

WELL I THINK MR. CALVIN IS VERY RUDE, DON'T YOU, MR. TIGER? YES, I THINK SO TOO. MORE TEA, ANYONE?

HEY, I SHOULD TELL SUSIE TO KEEP HER EYES OPEN FOR HOBBES.

SUSIE, I... HOBBES!

YOU FOUND HOBBES! THANK YOU THANK YOU THANKYOUTHANKYOUTHANKY OUTHANKYOUTHANKYOUTHA

WELL! WASN'T MR. CALVIN A GENTLEMAN! I DO HOPE... HEY! WHO TOOK ALL THE COOKIES ?!?

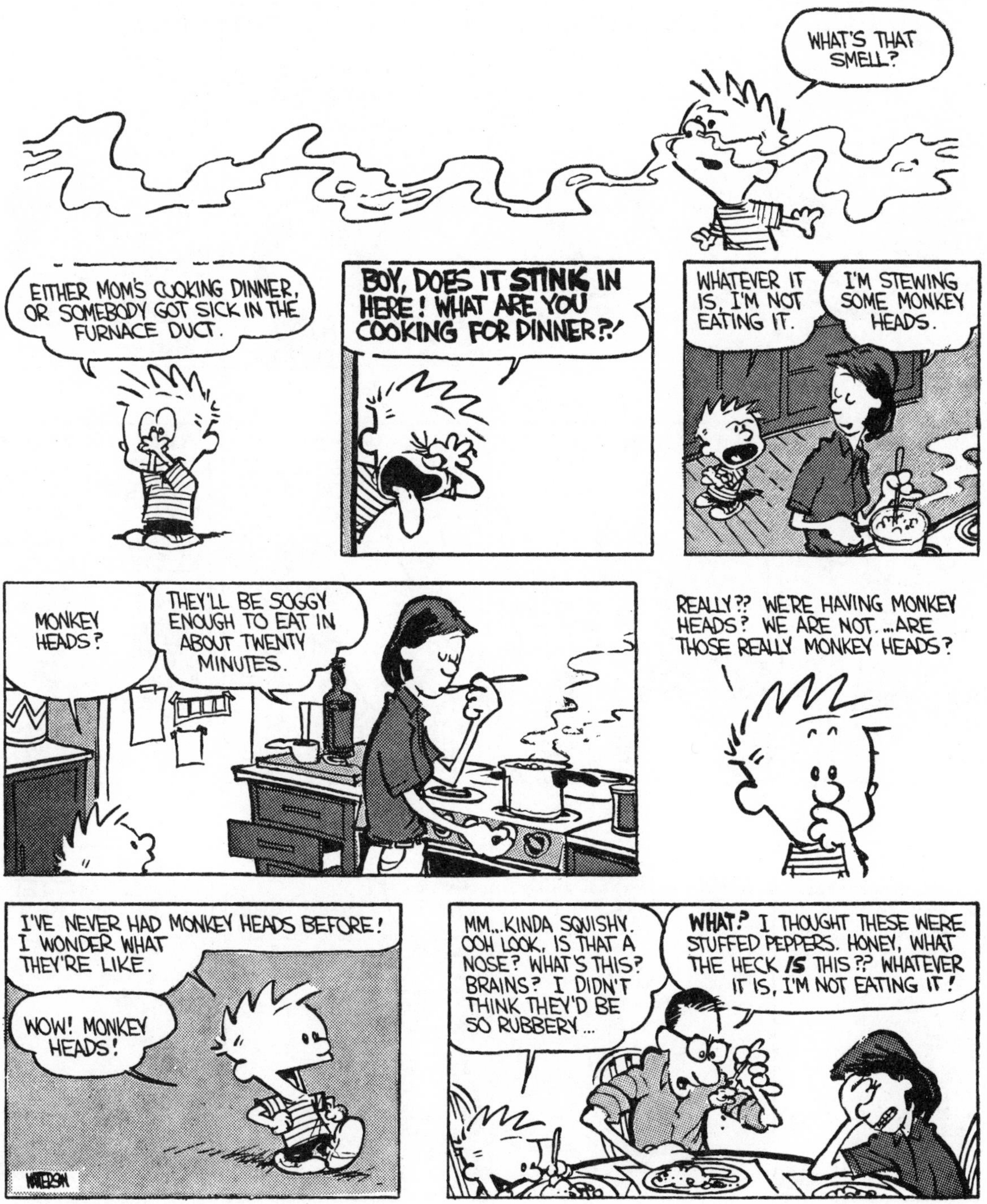
WHAT'S THAT SMELL?
EITHER MOM'S COOKING DINNER, OR SOMEBODY GOT SICK IN THE FURNACE DUCT.
BOY, DOES IT STINK IN HERE! WHAT ARE YOU COOKING FOR DINNER?!
WHATEVER IT IS, I'M NOT EATING IT.
I'M STEWING SOME MONKEY HEADS.
MONKEY HEADS?
THEY'LL BE SOGGY ENOUGH TO EAT IN ABOUT TWENTY MINUTES.
REALLY?? WE'RE HAVING MONKEY HEADS? WE ARE NOT. ...ARE THOSE REALLY MONKEY HEADS?
I'VE NEVER HAD MONKEY HEADS BEFORE! I WONDER WHAT THEY'RE LIKE.
WOW! MONKEY HEADS!
WATTERSON
MM...KINDA SQUISHY. OOH LOOK, IS THAT A NOSE? WHAT'S THIS? BRAINS? I DIDN'T THINK THEY'D BE SO RUBBERY...
WHAT? I THOUGHT THESE WERE STUFFED PEPPERS. HONEY, WHAT THE HECK IS THIS?? WHATEVER IT IS, I'M NOT EATING IT!

SUSIE, WANNA HEAR A SECRET?

SURE.

I THINK THE PRINCIPAL IS A SPACE ALIEN SPY.

HE'S TRYING TO CORRUPT OUR YOUNG INNOCENT MINDS SO WE'LL BE UNABLE TO RESIST WHEN HIS PEOPLE INVADE EARTH!

PROMISE NOT TO TELL ANYONE?

DON'T WORRY.

HOBBES, WHAT SHOULD I DO WHEN MOE COMES TO BEAT ME UP IN GYM CLASS?

WELL, YOU CAN ALWAYS DO WHAT WE TIGERS DO WHEN A RHINO CHARGES.

WHAT'S THAT?

WE SCRAMBLE LIKE MANIACS FOR THE NEAREST TREE.

THAT'S YOUR ADVICE?? TO SIT IN A TREE ALL DAY?!?

IT DOESN'T IMPRESS THE GIRLS, OF COURSE, BUT THERE'S NO SENSE IMPRESSING THEM AND THEN GETTING KILLED, MY DAD USED TO SAY...

HOBBES, I NEED YOUR HELP. THAT BULLY MOE KEEPS PUSHING ME AROUND.

...SO I WANT YOU TO COME TO SCHOOL AND EAT HIM, OK?

EAT HIM?

SURE! TIGERS EAT PEOPLE ALL THE TIME!

WHAT IF THE CAFETERIA LADIES WON'T LET ME USE THE OVEN?

HERE, CALVIN, I'LL SHOW YOU A MAGIC TRICK.

SEE? I PULLED A DIME FROM YOUR EAR! PRETTY GOOD, HUH?

ANYTHING YET?

J-JUST A B-B-BLOODY N-NOSE.

POOF
POOF
POOF

POW!

GOOD HEAVENS, I THINK I BLEW MY FACE INSIDE OUT!

98

THE WATER'S TOO COLD!

NOW IT'S TOO HOT.

NOW IT'S TOO COLD.

NOW IT'S TOO DEEP.

THE FEARSOME SHARK SENSES DISTRESS IN THE WAVES ABOVE HIM!

HE CIRCLES UP, CLOSER AND CLOSER TO THE TERRIFIED VICTIM!

HEY! YAHH! SNAP THRASH SNAP!

YOU KNOW, FOR SOMEONE WHO HATES BATHS AS MUCH AS YOU DO, YOU'RE NOT MAKING THIS GO ANY FASTER!

ANOTHER GRUESOME KILL..

EVERYBODY I KNOW HAS EITHER CABLE TV OR A VCR! THEY CAN WATCH ANYTHING THEY WANT!

BUT ME? *I* HAVE TO WATCH DUMB OL' SUMMER REPEATS! *I* HAVE TO WATCH THE SAME GARBAGE OVER AND OVER!

HOW CRUELLY WE MISTREAT YOU, CALVIN.

...SO THEN HE GAVE ME "OLIVER TWIST" TO READ, AND SAID I MIGHT IDENTIFY WITH IT.

RATS...AND "SORORITY ROW HORROR" IS ON CABLE TONIGHT.

I GOT A HELIUM BALLOON.

VERY NICE.

I'M GOING TO STAND ON THIS LADDER AND LET THE BALLOON CARRY ME UP AND AWAY.

NOTHING'S HAPPENING.

TRY JUMPING.

SEE? THERE GOES THE BALLOON. YOU DIDN'T HANG ON.

FLUSH!

WHEEE! HA HA HA!

I'M DONE WITH MY BATH.

MM... THAT WAS QUICK.

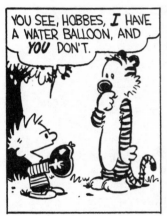

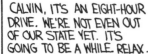

THAT TRIP WAS EXCRUCIATING. THANK GOODNESS WE'RE HERE.

EIGHT HOURS CRAMMED IN A CAR WITH A HYPERACTIVE SIX-YEAR-OLD! WHAT AN ORDEAL!

WATERSON

WELL, NOW CALVIN CAN RUN AND SCREAM ALL HE LIKES. AHH, WHAT A GREAT LITTLE PLACE.

I'M BORED. WHEN ARE WE LEAVING?

YOU'RE BORED? WOULD YOU LIKE ME TO SHOW YOU HOW AN ANCHOR WORKS?

AHH! ANOTHER GLORIOUS SUNRISE, AND NOT A SOUL AROUND!

THIS IS THE LIFE! A BRISK SWIM AT DAWN, A MORNING OUT IN A BOAT...

...AND BY 9 A.M., I'M BACK WITH FRESHLY CAUGHT FISH FOR BREAKFAST! THE DAY'S HARDLY BEGUN! WHAT A VACATION!

WATERSON

UGH...I'VE SEEN CHEERIER FACES AT THE OFFICE!

YOU EAT YOUR DEAD ANIMALS. ALL I WANT IS SOME COFFEE.

WHY ISN'T THERE ANY TV UP HERE? I HATE THIS PLACE.

DAD, LOOK! I CAUGHT A FISH!

HEY, THAT'S A BIG ONE. I'LL SHOW YOU HOW TO CLEAN IT, AND WE'LL HAVE IT FOR DINNER.

WATERSON

"CLEAN IT"?

CUT OFF ITS HEAD AND GUT IT.

MMM! PASS ME ANOTHER OF THESE GREAT CHEESE SANDWICHES! HA HA, NO BONES IN **THESE**, RIGHT?

STOMP
STOMP
STOMP
STOMP

WHAP
WHAP
WHAP
WHAP

I DON'T *LIKE* FOOD COOKED OUT, DO YOU?

UGH. IT ALL TASTES THE SAME.

CRUNCH CRUNCH

FLOWERS ARE PRETTY STUPID.

SEE, IT'S A BRIGHT, SUNNY DAY OUT, RIGHT?

WELL, WITH THIS WATERING CAN, I CAN MAKE THEM THINK IT'S RAINING.

IT'S FUN TO MESS WITH THEIR MINDS.

THE EXPERIMENT HAS GONE HORRIBLY WRONG! CALVIN HAS MUTATED INTO A GIANT FLY!

HE ZIPS ABOUT IN PARASITIC HUNGER, SEARCHING FOR DECAYING FLESH!

AN UNBEARABLE STENCH FILLS THE AIR. THE HIDEOUS BUG ZEROES IN.

MMM! THIS MAKES ME HUNGRY!

DON'T BE GROSS. JUST TAKE OUT THE GARBAGE LIKE I ASKED YOU, WILL YOU PLEASE?

IT'S ANOTHER NEW MORNING FOR MR. MONROE. HE GLANCES AT THE NEWSPAPER HEADLINES OVER A CUP OF COFFEE, AND GETS IN HIS RED SPORTS CAR TO GO TO WORK.

LITTLE DOES HE REALIZE IT'S HIS LAST DAY ON THE FACE OF THE EARTH!

CALVIN DRINKS THE MAGIC ELIXIR AND BEGINS AN INCREDIBLE TRANSFORMATION!

INSTANTLY HE GROWS! BIGGER AND BIGGER! HIGHER AND HIGHER!

HE IS NOW OVER 300 FEET TALL! THE FORMULA IS A SUCCESS!

CALVIN, THE MIGHTY GIANT, GOES ON A TERRIBLE RAMPAGE, STRIKING FEAR INTO THE HEARTS OF THE POPULACE!

NOTHING CAN STOP HIM! IT'S PANIC IN THE STREETS! A TOWN LIES IN RUINS!

NO, I WON'T BUY YOU ANY MORE TOY CARS. I SAW YOU! YOU DELIBERATELY STOMPED ON THOSE!

WATTERSON

HI, CALVIN, WHAT ARE YOU DOING?

BIG IMPORTANT SECRET THINGS! GO AWAY! GET LOST!

ALL RIGHT, DANDELION HEAD! WHO CARES WHAT YOU DO ANYWAY!

WE'RE DOING GREAT THINGS. *WE'RE* HAVING FUN!

I THOUGHT WE WERE BORED OUT OF OUR SKULLS.

OH HUSH. YOU DON'T KNOW ANYTHING.

THAT STUPID CALVIN. HE'S SO MEAN.

ALL I TRY TO DO IS BE FRIENDS, AND HE TREATS ME LIKE I'M NOBODY.

WELL, WHO NEEDS JERKS LIKE HIM ANYWAY? I DON'T NEED HIM FOR A FRIEND. I CAN HAVE FUN BY MYSELF!

POOP.

SUSIE, HOBBES THOUGHT I WAS RUDE, SO I'M SORRY, AND YOU CAN COME PLAY WITH US IF YOU WANT.

THANKS, CALVIN. THAT'S REALLY NICE OF YOU.

OK, WE'LL PLAY HOUSE NOW. I'LL BE THE HIGH-POWERED EXECUTIVE WIFE, THE TIGER HERE CAN BE MY UNEMPLOYED, HOUSEKEEPING HUSBAND, AND YOU CAN BE OUR BRATTY AND BRAINLESS KID IN A DAY CARE CENTER.

THIS WAS *YOUR* IDEA, PEA BRAIN.

DON'T YOU TALK TO YOUR FATHER THAT WAY!

I'M OFF TO WALL STREET. DON'T WAIT UP.

120

LOOK AT THAT THING IN THE DIRT! IT MUST BE A FOSSIL!

I WONDER WHAT PECULIAR ANIMAL *THIS* WAS.

BUT IT'S NOT A BONE. IT MUST BE SOME PRIMITIVE HUNTING WEAPON OR EATING UTENSIL FOR CAVE MEN.

MAYBE IT HAD SOME RELIGIOUS FUNCTION.

THIS EXPLAINS WHY YOUR CLOTHES STAY ON THE FLOOR.

MAKING A SIGN?

I'M DECLARING THE CREEK BACK IN THE WOODS "CALVIN'S CREEK."

WHEN YOU DISCOVER SOMETHING, YOU'RE ALLOWED TO NAME IT AND PUT UP A SIGN.

Calvin's CREEK

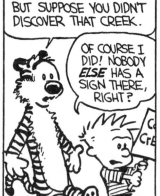

BUT SUPPOSE YOU DIDN'T DISCOVER THAT CREEK.

OF COURSE I DID! NOBODY *ELSE* HAS A SIGN THERE, RIGHT?

Hobs Crk

CAN HOBBES AND I GO PLAY IN THE RAIN, MOM?

NO.

WHY NOT?

YOU'LL GET SOAKED.

WHAT'S WRONG WITH THAT?

YOU COULD CATCH PNEUMONIA, RUN UP A TERRIBLE HOSPITAL BILL, LINGER A FEW MONTHS, AND DIE.

I ALWAYS FORGET. IF YOU ASK A MOM, YOU GET A WORST-CASE SCENARIO.

I HAD NO IDEA THESE LITTLE SHOWERS WERE SO *DANGEROUS.*

124

HERE COMES SUSIE.

HA! WON'T SHE BE HORRIFIED TO SEE HOW OUR FACES HAVE TRAGICALLY FROZEN!

HI, SUSIE.

HI, CALVIN.

WHAT DID YOU DO, GET YOUR HEAD STUCK IN THE BLENDER? IT'S AN IMPROVEMENT.

ARE THE COALS HOT?

YES, THEY'RE VERY HOT. I'M JUST ABOUT TO PUT ON THE HAMBURGERS.

BEFORE YOU DO, COULD YOU TOSS IN THE CAN OF LIGHTER FLUID AND MAKE A GIANT FIREBALL?

I'VE GOT THE MOST BORING DAD IN THE WORLD.

WITH THESE SNORKELS, WE CAN STAY UNDER WATER INDEFINITELY.

JUST THINK OF ALL THE FISH WE'LL BE ABLE TO SEE!

WE CAN COLLECT SHELLS!

LET'S GO!

WELL SO FAR, THIS HAS BEEN A MAJOR DISAPPOINTMENT

126

Finis